Buried Lies

True Tales and Tall Stories
from the PGA Tour

PETER JACOBSEN
with Jack Sheehan

G. P. Putnam's Sons
New York

G. P. Putnam's Sons
Publishers Since 1838
200 Madison Avenue
New York, NY 10016

Library of Congress Cataloging-in-Publication Data
Jacobsen, Peter.
    Buried lies : true tales and tall stories from the PGA tour /
Peter Jacobsen with Jack Sheehan
        p.   cm.
    ISBN 0-399-13810-2
        1. Jacobsen, Peter.   2. Golfers—United States—Biography.
3. Golf—Tournaments.   4. PGA Tour (Association)   I. Sheehan, Jack.
II. Title.
GV964.J33A3   1993   92-42827 CIP
796.352'092—dc20
[B]

Printed in the United States of America
8   9   10

This book is printed on acid-free paper.
∞

Contents

"Fore-Mative Years": The Family Jacobsen

IN MY SEVENTEEN YEARS on the PGA Tour, I've done hundreds of newspaper and magazine interviews, and because I enjoy telling a good anecdote, and usually have a lot of things to get off my chest, I've often been told that I should consider doing a book someday.

I undertook this project not because of my playing record—I certainly have not stamped my place in golf history the way many of the champions in these pages have—but I have had some great experiences, many funny moments, and done a few things a professional golfer normally wouldn't do. So, of course, I chose one of the most hectic years of my life to undertake this project.

As this book was being written, my father, Erling, was approaching the end of an eight-year battle with cancer, but he remained a great cheerleader and a wonderful inspiration for us all. After his surgery in 1990, for instance, he insisted on being with his family in a downtown Portland warehouse to pose with me for an Apollo golf shaft ad campaign. Dad's golf swing and posture in the pictures are perfect. No one would know that we had to stop the session every few minutes so that Dad could sit down. He still had his stitches in.

Later, my brother, David, and sister, Susie, and I would sit down with Dad, and I would read him aloud many of the early chapter drafts from this book. He would laugh and nod approvingly.

A couple of days before he died, I picked up a golf club leaning against the wall and handed it to him. His hands went on the club like he'd been born with it, and it occurred to me to ask him one final question.

"Dad," I said, "what's the most important part of golf?"

He looked at me through his kind blue eyes and said, "A sense of humor."

I've tried to keep that in mind in the telling of these stories. It is to the spirit, courage, and humor of Erling Jacobsen that this book is dedicated.

I have wonderful memories of growing up in the golfing Jacobsen family. We not only all loved golf, but we were pretty competitive. At one point several years ago, the combined handicap of all the Jacobsens was 27. I was a plus-three, my brothers David and Paul were a plus-one and an eight, Dad was a five, and Mom and Susie were nines. If there had been a *Family Feud* golf tournament, the Jacobsens could have held their own.

How avid were we? We even built a putting green in our backyard. Dad and David did most of the work, because David was basically the family greenskeeper and maintenance man (fittingly, he owns a turf equipment business today), and when it was finally finished, it was darned good, better than many I've played on the Tour.

We had regular family putting tournaments, and I'd pretend that those testy five-footers were for more than family honor—they were always to win the Masters or the U.S. Open. I had no idea that I would actually get to play in those tournaments one day.

It was in the backyard that I also began to develop my impersonations of other players' swings—something I'm well known for today. Of course, I did Arnie and Jack, but I also did Sam Snead, George Knudson, Miller Barber, Don January—all the players that I watched on *Shell's Wonderful World of Golf* and the *CBS Golf Classic*. The prime motivation was to get the approval of my mother. She'd laugh really hard and tell me I was good at it, and so I'd spend even more time practicing in front of a mirror to make them better. I guess you could say I got hooked on golf and entertaining at about the same time.

I got my sense of humor from my dad, too. Dad loved practical jokes, especially in the morning. One time, our family rented a condominium at Black Butte Ranch, in eastern Oregon, for a week of golf and relaxation. The condo sat on the shore of a lake that was home to several large geese. On this particular morning, Dad was down feeding them bread crumbs when he got a wonderful idea: he'd employ the geese to wake us up. So he lured them up to the house with the old Hansel-and-Gretel routine. He sprinkled a trail of breadcrumbs all the way up to the deck, through the sliding-glass door into the condo, and right up to the door of the bedroom where David and I were dead to the world.

Dad then opened the door and threw the rest of the bread onto our beds. I woke up to a gaggle of long-necked geese snapping at bread bits all over me. It was like Alfred

Hitchcock's *The Birds* . . . only the birds were on steroids. David and I jumped out of bed screaming, and this in turn scared the hell out of the geese, who went honking back out into the living room. They flew toward the light of day, which was right into the glass door. They weren't hurt, only stunned, but after another second they freaked out and started flapping and squawking and got themselves tangled in the curtains. This made them even more panicky, and their bowels came totally uncorked. Instantly, goose crap was everywhere, and Mom was having a fit, and David and Dad and I were laughing hysterically. We finally got them outside without any major injuries, but over the next few days there was some serious carpet-and-drape cleaning going on.

One of the great things about learning golf from my father is that he appreciated how important the game was in shaping personality. He would always take one or more of us kids to the course with him, and would often include us in his foursome. I played several times with Mr. Bill Knight, the father of Nike founder Phil Knight, and Mr. Peter Murphy, of the Murphy lumber family in Portland. You notice I still call them *Mister*—it's the only way I can think of them. They were older than my father, almost two generations removed from me, and they were classy, distinguished gentlemen. I was able to form different attitudes and thoughts about the world by playing with them, rather than just with kids my own age. I felt I really had to have my act together when I was with these men, because they had such respect for the game. They also showed *me* respect, and at my age that was special.

My father was a stickler for golf course etiquette. Not

only did he always replace his divots, but on par-three holes he'd always pick up four or five others and meticulously lay them down and step on them. He'd fit in each divot as if it was the most important piece of a jigsaw puzzle. He didn't care if it was just a little nip of grass or a pelt that looked like it came from Sy Sperling's Hair Club for Men; Dad would carefully replace it and sometimes even secure it by sticking a tee in it.

One time, I was scolded by a close family friend, Mr. R. S. Miller, after hitting three or four shots to a green at Waverley Country Club, my home club. Mr. Miller made the point emphatically that practice was for the driving range, not the golf course. When I got home, I assumed Dad would give me sympathy and support, but he didn't. He said that Mr. Miller was right, and that I should have known better. It taught me something about conviction. I realized that Dad had greater respect for the etiquette of the game than for my damaged pride.

Then when I got a little older, about twelve, I perfected this great tantrum move. I'd tee the ball up, give one waggle, take my backswing, pause at the top, swing as hard as I could, and if it was a bad shot I'd instantly reverse the swing and bury the club back into the ground with a loud *Whop*. This was most effective on tee-shots, because the driver would leave an impression in the ground like a muddy horseshoe print. My patented reverse slam would put such stress on the shaft that once or twice the club ended up looking like a damn hockey stick.

I'd usually accompany this move with a chorus of four-letter action verbs, most of which I didn't understand, and all of which I was years away from performing. If I were to make an analogy, I was like Spalding, the spoiled nephew in *Caddyshack*—you know, the fat kid who burps, passes gas, picks his nose, and uses foul language. It's the difficult adolescent zone into which some kids fall, when you're incorrigible and you don't know why.

Finally, my horrible golf etiquette caught up with me— and taught me a valuable lesson. I was playing with my father and David and another friend at the Astoria Country Club. We were on the tee of the 7th hole, a par-four. I followed my normal routine of waggle, swing, follow-through, bad-shot, *Whop.* My driver embedded in the ground and I screamed an obscenity.

"That's it, Peter!" my dad said. "If you cannot act like a gentleman, you can't play any more golf today."

He took my clubs and told me to go back and sit in the car while they finished the round as a threesome.

So I stomped off and said, "Fine, fine!" It was a long walk back to the clubhouse, and it took me over hill and dale, over a sand dune, through a fairway, over another dune, and through another fairway.

By the time I got to the car, I was even more angry and frustrated, and hating life. I remember sitting there in the car in a stunned silence, thinking how I had embarrassed myself.

I couldn't go into the clubhouse because the guys would have asked why I wasn't still playing, so I didn't have much choice but to sit there and let it all sink in. At that age, kids think that their parents are put on earth only to serve their needs, and that their parents don't have feelings and don't have sex, and . . . well . . . that incident put a few things in perspective for me. Here was this beautiful day, on a wonderful course near the ocean, and my behavior had forced me to stop playing and sit all by myself in a hot car for two hours.

The fact that I remember the incident so vividly reveals what an important lesson it was. (Note: I have not repeated the *Whop* move since that day, but I have muttered a few choice words. Under my breath, of course.)

I got another lesson at about the same time, when I played in a pro-junior tournament at Tualatin Country Club, paired with Jon Peterson, the assistant pro at Waverley.

I was about twelve or thirteen, and I'd never broken 40 for nine holes, but this day I shot a 46 on the front nine—and on the back nine drained everything: I had ten putts for the nine holes and shot 39. I won Low Net for the tournament, and Jon raved about what a great putter and clutch player I was—he talked about my performance as though he were describing Chip Beck shooting his 59.

On the drive back to Astoria, where we were spending the summer, I couldn't wait to show the trophy to my parents. We stopped somewhere along the way for dinner, and all the kids were still talking about my great round, and I was jamming food in my mouth as fast as I could and lapping up the praise like a pack mule at a water trough.

Then disaster struck: we got in the car to finish the ride and I realized I'd lost my bite plate for my braces, that horrendous-looking slab of membrane that always had fuzz and bits of ol' Life Savers stuck to it from being in my pocket all day rather than in my mouth. We stopped and turned on the interior lights and searched the car, but it was nowhere to be found. The defining moment of my youth suddenly turned to ashes, and I ended up crying in my brother David's arms, fearful I was going to get my butt kicked for losing yet another in a series of elusive, thirty-eight-dollar bite plates.

But this was the lesson: when we got home, my parents were more interested in my personal-best 39 than in the tooth-straightener. They were as excited for me as I had been. As I said, the Jacobsen family loves golf . . . far more than orthodontics. It was then that I got the notion in the back of my mind that maybe I could go somewhere in this game, and I've never looked back.

It was after that first bath of adoration that I got almost ritualistic about golf, going so far as to clean the grooves of my clubs meticulously each night before a tournament round. I'd run a metal fingernail file carefully through the groove of each iron, and even in the numbers on the bottom of the club. Then I'd run hot water over the face of the irons until steam filled the room. I'd make sure the water was scalding when I did the putter, so that the blade would stay "hot" the next day and hole everything.

In *Wayne's World,* they would call me "mental." Personally, I think it's standard behavior for all golfers once they catch the bug.

One last lesson from my younger days.

I'm often asked by parents of junior golfers such things as what handicap their son should be at age fifteen, and how many junior tournaments I had won by the age of thirteen. I explain that timetables like that are pointless. What is important is that the girl or boy enjoy the game and learn the character-building lessons that golf can impart. Twelve-year-olds who have competed in a heavy tournament schedule since they were seven or eight often burn out early, which is a shame. And I frequently hear of parents who are greatly disappointed when their children don't live up to their unrealistic expectations. This is even more shameful. Golf is a recreation that can and should last a lifetime, regardless of the skill level of the participant.

When I talk with these parents, I point out that I hadn't won *any* tournaments by the time I was thirteen—and I was never the least bit upset about it. That's because, thanks to the influence of my father and men like him, I always placed as much importance on the enjoyment aspect of golf as on the competition. My father always asked me two things after a round of golf: "Did you have fun?" and "What did you learn out there?" As a result, I've tried never to get too solemn "out there," even when I'm competing at my hardest.

I've sometimes wondered whether that attitude hasn't hurt me at times, because I don't have quite the win-at-all-cost ethic of some other players. There's always that prankster side of me looking for the humor of every situation. But if my personality has cost me a title or two, I feel I've more than made up for it with laughter.

And I'd like to share some of that laughter with you now . . .

CHAPTER 1

Across the Pond

I'VE PLAYED IN THREE major championships at the Old Course at St. Andrews, and each has been filled with wonder and excitement. They've had a mystical aura to them because of my feelings about the essence of golf and the game's rich history.

My first visit was in 1976 to play in the British Amateur championship. My decision to play had been based solely on the venue. I wanted to experience the Old Course before I turned professional, while I was still what the British call a "simon pure."

The trip didn't make sense economically, because I knew I was going to be married later in the year, but I've never based important decisions on money. I reasoned that competing at St. Andrews was tremendously important to my growth as a player and as a person, and therefore would make me a better husband once I was married (which shows we can rationalize almost anything if we want to do it badly enough).

I arrived in Scotland early in the morning. I was so

excited, and wired from jet lag, that when I got to the town of St. Andrews I walked around to soak up the atmosphere. I had an immediate sense of history, from the cobblestone streets to a tour through St. Andrews Castle. It was a whole other world to me.

For an Oregon college kid used to McDonald's and Dunkin' Donuts for breakfast, it was neat to see a horse-drawn milk wagon making its morning rounds. I stopped the driver and bought a quart from him. The bottle didn't even have a top on it, just a thick layer of cream. Then I went to a bakery and introduced myself to several townspeople, who were friendly and warm. I told them why I was there, and they were impressed that I had come all that way to play in their amateur championship. While I didn't sense that any of them were golfers, it was obvious they had a great deal of civic pride over the fact that their hometown was a shrine to all who loved the game. The owner gave me warm donuts and pastries, and wouldn't take any money for them. Others gave me tips on local customs and—something I found delightfully surprising—they all had their own ideas about how to play the infamous 17th hole at St. Andrews, known as the Road Hole. More about that later.

Later in the morning, I checked into the bed-and-breakfast near the golf course, the kind with shared bathroom quarters. It was no big deal after the fraternity at the University of Oregon. Any notion of privacy is abandoned after you've hung with the "brothers" a few years.

When I checked in at the Old Course, I was pleased to learn I had been assigned Michael Bonallack's regular caddy. Michael is a highly esteemed player, and the current secretary of the Royal and Ancient Golf Club. A five-time winner of the British Amateur, he's also made many Walker Cup appearances.

My caddy's name was Sydney B. Rutherford, and he was seventy years old and came up to about my armpit. A spryer, wittier leprechaun you'll never find. His brogue was thicker than the heather that blooms in the St. Andrews rough, and nearly everything he said made me laugh. When we were first introduced, he said, "Hae na fair, wee Syd is hair."

"Excuse me?" I said, and leaned closer to try to decipher his message. When he repeated the line, I realized he was saying "Have no fear, wee Syd is here."

And so it went all week. Although everything Sydney B. Rutherford said was difficult to understand, it was well worth bending an ear for.

In the first practice round, for instance, I hit my drive off the first tee, and when we reached the ball I started pacing all around. After a moment, wee Syd said, "What ur ya luckin' fer, Pee-air?"

I told him a sprinkler head, so I could walk off a yardage (I didn't know then there was no irrigation system at St. Andrews). He looked at me, set the bag down, and said, "Yardage? Nay, you donna wan no yardage on the ol' gurl. If ya need ta know how fer it is, I'll tell ya."

Later that day, on the 13th hole, a long and difficult par-four, the wind was at our back and Syd had me hit an eight-iron from 175 yards, which ended up pin-high. The next morning, on the same hole, the wind was dead in our face and I had about 200 yards to the flag. Now, on the back nine at St. Andrews, all the holes head into the clubhouse, and because many of the shots are blind the golfer must aim at various buildings in the town or landmarks on the horizon. So Syd told me to aim at the steeple of the church. Then he pulled the sock off my three-wood and handed it to me. I thought it was way too much club and told him so.

He glared back at me. "Pee-air, I tell ya it's a three-wood," he said, "and donna leave nonuv it hair."

I laughed and ripped it, and sure enough when we came over the rise and could see the green, the ball was pin-high, 15 feet away. I remember thinking, this guy is a national treasure. I'm gonna tuck him into the ball pocket of my golf bag and smuggle him back to the States. The only drawback was that I would have had to put a set of head-phones on like they use at the United Nations, so an interpreter could tell me what the hell he was saying.

Another day, at the 15th hole, wee Syd did something unusual, and I realized that he'd done it the previous day as well. He left my side and walked to the right, taking an unnecessarily long route to the green. So I asked him why, and he said, "Aye, Laddie, I want to pae tribute to Madame Graziano."

He told me that the two mounds on the side of the fairway are called—ready?—Madame Graziano's Tits, and that respectful golfers always walk between them to get to the green. Now I don't know whether Madame Graziano was a woman for whom he had caddied, or someone he knew from a sport played in darker quarters than golf, but she must have been quite a gal, judging by the size of those mounds.

Each time I've returned to St. Andrews, I look up wee Sydney. He's in his eighties now, but he still has all the wit and charm he possessed when I first met him.

My next competition at St. Andrews was in the 1984 British Open, and once again I was tremendously excited to be there. I was so pumped up that I shot a 67 in the first round, and held a share of the lead with Greg Norman and British professional Bill Longmuir. That was the year that a bad bounce on the infamous 17th hole, the Road Hole, cost Tom Watson a chance at the title, which went to Seve Ballesteros. Little did I know the spectrum of emotions I would go through the next time I played that hole, in 1990. But I'll arrive at that in a jiffy, as Sydney would say.

I remember having a lot of fun in the press conference following the opening round in '84. It was my first time in front of most of the British writers, and recognizing their appreciation of wit and irony, I wanted to give them something a little different from the routine post-round re-hash of a good score: driver, six-iron, 15-footer, yawn, snooze . . .

I had recently read the book *Golf in the Kingdom,* by writer Michael Murphy. It's the story of a young American golfer named Michael, who travels through Great Britain on his way to India to study philosophy and religion. While in Britain, he plays a round of golf at a course called Burningbush, patterned after St. Andrews, and meets an enchanting older professional named Shivas Irons, who astounds Michael with his golfing ability and wisdom. The story contains elements of Zen, magic, psychology, and history, and is an irresistible read for anyone who loves the game of golf. I had been introduced to the brilliance of the book by Chuck Hogan, a friend and golf educator who founded Sports Enhancement Associates, and has been a marvelous teacher to me through the years.

The characters in *Golf in the Kingdom* reaffirm everything I believe about the beauty of the sport and its interplay of mind, soul, and body. It also contains many poetic descriptions that have stayed with me long afterward, such as: "The thrill of seeing a ball fly over the countryside, over obstacles—especially over a stretch of water—and then onto the green and into the hole has a mystic quality. What is it but the flight of the alone to the alone?"

Or "Ye're makin' a mistake if ye think the gemme [game] is meant for the shots. The gemme is for walkin' . . . Tis a rotten shame, for if ye can enjoy the walkin' ye can probably enjoy the other times in yer life when ye're *in between*. And that's most o' the time, wouldn't ye say?"

Anyway, it was as though a window of awareness had been opened to me when I read the book, so I was eager to discuss its influence in the press room at St. Andrews. In talking about my 67, I quoted Shivas Irons and his teacher, Seamus Macduff. I was also so overcome by the venerability of the course, and the spirits of all those who had played there before me, that I alluded to the movie *Ghostbusters*, which was a big hit at the time. "I saw so many ghosts floating over the landscape out there," I said, "that I was afraid I was going to get 'slimed.' "

Some of the writers laughed, but the others looked at me like my porchlight had burned out. Then the ghosts themselves decided to teach me a lesson for taking them so lightly.

First, they fixed me for the rest of the tournament: I closed with three straight 73s. I still finished 22nd and enjoyed the week tremendously, but the British press was probably relieved that they could get back to reporting birdies and bogies instead of Zen masters and apparitions.

Then the spirits lay in wait for my return . . .

I was more than normally pumped up for the British Open when it returned to St. Andrews in 1990. I was in the midst of my best-ever season in the U.S., with a win at the Bob Hope Desert Classic, third-place finishes at the L.A. Open and Western Open, and two other top-tens, so when I arrived in Scotland I was brimming with confidence.

For the first 54 holes, my game plan was working perfectly. I was eight under par after the third round, and although not about to catch Nick Faldo, who was running away with the tournament at 17 under, I was in solid contention for a top-five finish. Plus, I was really enjoying the experience. Playing a great course in a major championship is a thrill all its own, but to play well to boot is the best feeling you can have as a professional golfer.

It got even more fun through 10 holes of the final round, as I made four birdies and an eagle going out, and worked myself into third place at 14 under par. With the wind whipping harder by the minute, I bogied three of the next six holes, but others were dropping strokes to par also, so I was still tied for fourth as I came to the Road Hole.

I'm willing to relive that hole for you now because I think what happened to me there epitomizes the fickleness of golf, and how the golfing gods can spit in your eye at a moment's notice.

I should further preface the impending horror by reporting that I had birdied the Road Hole the previous day, holing a meandering putt of about 95 feet. When the putt finally dissolved into the cup, I darted across the green like Neon Deion Sanders returning a punt for a touchdown. The exhibition of glee was caught by BBC cameras and beamed back to the U.S. on ABC. Perhaps, in retrospect, I should have been more subdued, because I obviously insulted Harry Vardon and Old Tom Morris and all those other hovering presences that lurked in the gorse at St. Andrews.

Anyway, there I was on Sunday afternoon, about to finish my best-ever British Open as I stood on the 17th tee. Now, there's just no way to emphasize how difficult that hole is. The tee-shot, for starters, is totally blind. Your target is over a replica of an ancient railway shed, over the hotel grounds, and into a fairway that makes an extreme dogleg to the right. You just pray your ball lands in the fairway, because the out-of-bounds wall is close by and the rough is potluck: sometimes you can play out of it, other times your ball sinks deeper than the Titanic. The hole plays to 480 yards, and while it's a par-four, it's tougher than three-quarters of all the par-fives in the U.S. I believe it's the hardest hole in golf, tougher even than the 16th at Cypress Point, simply because there are so many different hazards that can grab you by the throat and choke the life out of you.

Off the tee, you have thick gorse and long grass to the left, and the out-of-bounds to the right. These are scarier than normal because you can't see any of the trouble—you just know it's there. To the right and running behind the green is an old city road that gives the hole its name. Behind the road is a stone wall against which many balls come to rest, leaving either an unplayable lie or a bank shot that would even give Minnesota Fats difficulty—even if he were skinny. It was by this wall that Tom Watson met his doom in 1984.

It's almost like Dante's Inferno: the further down the hole you get, the more horrifying it becomes. I'm referring particularly to the pot bunker that fronts the left side of the green. It is known as the Sands of Nakajima, from an episode that occurred in the 1978 Open. The fine Japanese professional, Tommy Nakajima, hit the green in regulation, putted the ball off the green into the bunker, then took three futile swipes from the pit before finally flopping it onto the green and two-putting for a nine.

I've always wondered how a scorer keeping stats in that group would have charted that hole. Let's see: hit fairway, hit green, one putt, bunker shot, bunker shot, bunker shot, bunker shot, putt, putt, vomit. The scorer would go through three no. 2 pencils and a felt-tipped pen to get it all down.

I'd like to think that when the scorer asked Tommy what he had on the hole, he said he'd just send in an estimate, but I imagine he was too busy taking smelling salts to respond.

Anyway, I remember hitting my drive solidly down the left side that day. There was a strong left-to-right wind, so the play was to favor the left side to avoid the out-of-bounds right. When we got to the ball, I saw the wind hadn't moved it enough and I was about five yards off the fairway in the beach grass, sometimes called "love" grass. I can think of far more appropriate descriptions for it: like "horseshit."

It *is* possible to draw a good lie in that stuff. In fact, earlier in the tournament, from my hotel room which overlooked that fairway, I'd seen Faldo hit it in the left rough twice, draw good lies both times, and both times hit it onto the green. Apparently, the golf gods decided I needed to build some more character, because that wasn't an option for me. My ball settled deeper than a marble in a shag carpet. Although I had 220 yards to the green, my only hope was to try to chop it out and slightly forward with an eight-iron. A score of four was now out of the question. I just wanted to make five, and—as Ken Venturi loves to say—walk quietly to the next tee.

From the time I swung at that ball, everything seemed to shift into slow motion, almost as though it were happening in a dream, or shall we say nightmare. It was like the fight sequence from *Rocky*. I could almost read the lettering and number on the ball as it popped straight up and went over my left shoulder about six yards. I was now deeper in the rough and had actually lost yardage.

I was more shocked and embarrassed than angry. I thought, Holy Moly, I'm a professional. I can do better than that. I turned to my caddie, Mike, and said simply, "Wow!"

And Mike said, recognizing the severity of the predicament, "Let's just get this thing out of here."

I put the eight-iron back and grabbed a pitching wedge. Again, I was just trying to get it back in the short grass. Meanwhile, my playing partner, Nick Price, was waiting patiently in the fairway.

So I went after my third shot with the pitching wedge, and the ball did the exact same thing. It went about 10 yards and directly left. I was getting deeper by the swipe.

Now there were probably four or five thousand people in the bleachers on the back of the green and along the fairway and they were watching this like a presentation of *Macbeth*. There was a lot of blood being spilled, but no one could take his eyes off it.

I'm certain there were some snickers in the crowd, because in that heavy grass the ball has a mind of its own. I'd swung hard twice and the ball had just popped like a jumping bean behind me. It's funny to me even now, but I wasn't exactly splitting a rib at the time. I was seeing a great British Open getting devoured in the weeds.

For my fourth shot, I went with the sand wedge, and the good news was that I finally got the club under the ball, and got it airborne. The bad news is that it went further left, into even deeper hay.

Poor Nicky Price was watching this from the fairway like a man standing on a sidewalk staring up at a guy in a burning building: feeling horrible for him, but knowing there's not a thing he can do, and thanking God at the same time that it's not him up there.

I motioned for Nick to go ahead, and he hit his second

shot as I waded in to try to slash it out in five. This time, I finally got back to the fairway, and my reaction was to raise my arms in mock surprise and wave them in the air. I guess I was telling the stunned crowd that they could clap now, or cry now, and take their children home and tuck them in and assure them that the sun would rise again tomorrow.

I remember seeing the face of one older man, who wore a wry smile, and he was politely clapping for me. If I could put that smile into words, it would say something like, "Aye, the poor bastard's getting it oop the ars-el on the Road-el. Next time eel know to stae oot-a the garden."

I caught my sixth shot a little heavy and it came up short of the green. And as I walked up to hit my seventh, I flashed back to the day before and how great I had felt running across the green to pick that monster birdie putt out of the hole. I had to smile at the fickle fortunes of golf. I told Mike, "Ya know, yesterday I pissed off the legends, and today they're gathered by the hearth with a pint of Guinness laughing at me."

I didn't feel like pouting. I just felt totally humbled. Looking back, it was probably the most disappointing single golf hole I've ever played, because it knocked me out of the top five to a tie for 16th in the world's oldest tournament on the world's most revered golf course. It all ended somewhat positively, though. I hit my pitch shot over the bunker to about 10 feet from the cup, and holed the putt for an eight.

I thought of the old joke: Question: "How in the world did you make an *eight* on that hole?"

Answer: "I sunk a ten-footer."

When the putt went in, I took off my visor and made a deep bow to the crowd, and they gave me a big ovation. A lot of heads were cocked in sympathy. As Shivas Irons says, "Gowf is a way o' makin' a man naked," and I've probably never felt more exposed than at that very moment. I didn't know whether to laugh or cry or just run off into the undergrowth like a screaming banshee.

As frustrating as that experience was, it's also a poignant memory and one that gives me a sense of pride as well. Because through it all, I never lost my cool and was able to smile and laugh at myself and at the situation. If you're not able to do that at golf, no matter how tough it gets, you're missing the point of the game.

The one consoling factor about making that putt for eight was that I was able to trim the "Sands of Nakajima" by one stroke and escape the humility of having the left rough forever named in my honor as "The Beater of Peter," or "The Wake of Jake."

I'm certain when Shivas made his comment about golf making you naked, however, he didn't have in mind anything like the scene that occurred at Royal St. George's on the last hole of the British Open in 1985.

I was in contention after three rounds that year, and was paired with Tom Kite in the third-to-last pairing. Right behind us was Sandy Lyle, who would win the tournament.

The final hole at Royal St. George's is a difficult par-four, and tough to reach in two into the big wind we were facing. I was in the right front junk, preparing to pitch on, when the most astonishing event transpired: one of the marshals behind the green ripped off his coat, bolted from the gallery, and started running buck-naked around the green. He ran from the back of the green and circled around from the left side, around in front of me and to the back again. The people laughed and cheered, and Kite and

I had a chuckle as the streaker got a second wind and did another lap. He wasn't happy with a 440; he wanted to do an 880. Well, it ceased to be funny as Lord Godiva completed that circuit and carried on to the mile run, because he was tromping on my line.

So the third time around, here came the bobbies, with the nightsticks and the whistles and those great hats with the chinstraps. One hand is on the hat and the other is on the whistle. There were now about six people on the green, five with shoes and one without. The elapsed time of the run was about a minute, and I started to wonder if this could be the son of Roger Bannister. I mean, the guy was really striding. Then I remembered Sandy Lyle back in the fairway trying to win the British Open, and I got angry for the intrusion. It had gotten way out of hand.

On the guy's fourth lap, he starting running right at Kite. Tom quickly backed out of the way, not overly eager to have a close encounter with this fruitcake. I wasn't ecstatic about the idea myself, but the guy just wouldn't stop.

So as he ran toward me, I got down in my best Lawrence Taylor stance and put a couple head-jukes on him to let him know I was ready for contact. I remembered from playing tackle football as a kid that you didn't look at a runner's head or eyes, you aimed for his midsection. So when the guy got about five feet from me, I lowered my shoulder and dove at his hips. I made certain I turned my head at the last minute, so I wouldn't end up with a mouth full of parsley.

It was a clean hit, and as I drove him to the green I could hear the wind rush out of him. About this time, the bobbies scurried over and dogpiled him, and led him off the green. One bobbie had his hat hiding the guy's frontal area, and another his backside. The crowd was going nuts, and

I realized what it must feel like to make the winning tackle in the Ohio State/Michigan game.

As long as play was being held up anyway, I did a Mark Gastineau sack dance. I don't know what came over me, but I held up my thumb and index finger about an inch apart, to let the fans know that this guy literally was no big deal.

The next day, sure enough, most of the U.S. newspapers and many of the British papers ran the streaker's picture on page one, and poor Sandy Lyle's victory had to take second billing.

No matter what happens with the rest of my career, I know there is one statistical category on the Tour in which I will always be number one, and that is Leading Tacklers. I have one, and everybody else is tied for second with none.

CHAPTER 2

Nice Shot!

IN MY SEVENTEEN YEARS on the Tour, I've seen an untold number of great shots and great rounds. But there are a few that stand out as being really special—either because of the player involved or the circumstances of the day. One was Bob Tway's bunker shot to beat Greg Norman in the 1986 PGA, which I'll get to in another chapter. In terms of the impact it had on those two golfers' careers, that was probably the most important shot I've witnessed up close.

Earlier that same year, however, I was privileged to watch a final-round stretch run that I'll be able to tell my grandkids about. It grew as those things do, with one great shot building on another, and it drove the fans into a frenzy that you rarely see in golf.

It was a case of the greatest golfer of all time turning it on in front of his home-town fans, in a tournament he'd founded and on a course he'd designed himself. I'm talking about Jack Nicklaus playing in the Memorial Tournament at Muirfield Village in Columbus, Ohio.

The context and the surroundings are what made it

special. Just a few weeks before, as most golf fans remember, Nicklaus had shot the greatest final nine holes of his career to win the Masters. At the age of forty-six and at a time when most writers considered Jack too old to capture another major title, he had shot 30 on the back side at Augusta National to win his sixth Masters and twentieth major championship. It was certainly the crowning achievement in an incredible career, and nothing Jack could ever do would top it. The fact that his son Jackie had been caddying for him added a special dimension to the victory.

It was just a month later that I was paired in the final round of the Memorial with Jack and Andy Bean, who two years before had lost a playoff to Nicklaus at the same tournament. We had an immense gallery, but then they'd flock to watch Jack at Muirfield if he were playing in a blind-bogey tournament on a Monday with the juniors six-hole group. In Ohio, Nicklaus would win a popularity contest over a parley card of Mother Teresa, Johnny Carson, and Elvis back from the dead. And many of the people who watch him there have followed him for forty years, from his boyhood in Columbus, to his college days at Ohio State, through his incredible pro career.

That week at Muirfield in 1986 had the effect of a victory lap for Nicklaus, as the excitement of his Masters win was still fresh in everyone's memory. Every move he made drew applause. They cheered when he took off his glove.

Anyway, none of us had generated much excitement on the front nine of that final round. We were all about even-par. We were having a good time, and had a nice camaraderie among us, but it looked like we were just playing for position, because Hal Sutton had a big lead. Or so I thought until Nicklaus entered . . . the Twilight Zone.

On number 10, Jack hit a good drive and a six-iron 12 feet behind the hole and made it for birdie. On the 11th, a tricky par-five that is difficult to reach under less than perfect conditions, he got home in two with a drive and a one-iron, and two-putted for another birdie.

Number 12 is a par-three that is reminiscent of the 12th hole at Augusta. It's a pretty little jewel until it eats your lunch once or twice. Then, like the prom queen who loses her dentures when she bites into a cheeseburger, she never looks quite the same again. There's water short and right and the green's just a little sliver cut into the side of a hill. If you're overly cautious and hit it to the left, you land either in a bunker or on the hill, and getting it up and down from there is mission impossible. Too far right, you need fins and a snorkel. This day, the pin was cut back right, which is the most difficult spot. But Nicklaus went dead at it. He hit a beautiful cut seven-iron in there about 12 feet, and made the putt for his third birdie in a row. It was starting to get interesting.

With each birdie, the crowd screamed louder and the whole atmosphere got more electric. People abandoned other groups and rushed over to ours, as the leader board flashed the news that Jack was going deeper and deeper into the red.

Andy and I both started to play better as well, like cars in a stock-car race drafting the leader and getting pulled along in his vacuum.

After the birdie at 12, Jack was about four strokes behind Sutton, but he also knew that if he made a few more birdies he could post a number that might hold up. Nicklaus always analyzes the totals after 54 holes and picks a number he'll need to shoot in the final round to win. And after that birdie on the 12th, I could just sense that he was thinking of a number like 65.

On the 13th hole, a downhill par-four dogleg left, Jack hit a drive and a middle-iron about eight feet, and made it. Now he really had the "look"—intense but slightly glazed—that great players get when they're in a zone of perfect concentration. Ray Floyd gets it, as do Lanny and Curtis. At those times the fairways look wider, the hole looks bigger, and you just can't wait to get to the next shot because you know you'll hit it well. It's the way golf is played in Heaven.

The 14th hole at Muirfield Village is a truly spectacular par-four. It's short, only about 350 yards long, and calls for a precise shot off the tee for position, and then a short-iron to a tiny little green, with water guarding the right side. The pin that day was in the back right position, the toughest place they can put it.

I had hit my second shot into the left bunker, a tough spot from which to make par. Bean had hit his second about 12 feet from the hole, and Nicklaus about 15 feet. An amphitheater frames the left side of the 14th green, and all of Western civilization had gathered there to cheer on their man. They were yelling, "Go Jack" and "We love you, Jack." Andy and I might as well have been hawking programs and soft drinks for all we meant to the crowd at that moment.

One of the things I've learned on Tour is that I don't have to put my ego in check at a time like that, because the crowd does it for you. From playing so much with Palmer, I've gotten a master's degree in protocol when playing with a legend. I always give them their due respect, much like a rookie might do with a more experienced player. Respect is something you earn as a golfer, and not many players had earned more than Nicklaus. At the same time, I had a darned tough up-and-down facing me, so I didn't want to get so caught up in the adulation for Jack that I threw away my own round. Somehow, I hit a good bunker shot and it trickled down to about four feet from the hole.

Although Nicklaus was clearly away, Bean went up and set his ball down and putted first. I thought it was strange that Andy was playing out of turn, because I hadn't seen him and Jack communicate with each other. But Andy knocked it in and got a nice round of applause.

Immediately, people started yelling encouragement to Nicklaus again. I was standing next to Jack, just holding my ball and waiting for him to putt, when he turned to me and nonchalantly said, "Peter, do you want to go ahead and putt out?"

That really caught me off-guard, because you usually do that kind of thing only on the final hole of a tournament when you're saving the last putt for the winner. I looked at him and said, "Why would I putt out, Jack? You're away."

He replied, without any hesitation, "Because when I make this putt, the people here are going to go crazy."

I distinctly remember he said "when," and not "if."

Now, he had a 15-footer with about a nine-inch break from left to right. It was a darned tough putt. But I could tell from his eyes that he had absolutely no doubt that he was going to make it. He was merely offering me the courtesy of hitting my crappy little par putt before all hell broke loose.

Even though I sensed that he was right, that I should putt out, I said, "Jack, you go ahead, because I have to learn to deal with these types of situations."

And I remember Jackie Nicklaus, who was caddying for his dad and had his own aspirations as a player, nodding at me as if to say, yeah, that's all part of learning to play in the big leagues. Good move, Peter.

Then Jack hunched over his putt, and with the concentration of a safecracker leaning in to hear the tumblers click, he measured the line to the hole. Even with all those thousands of people surrounding the green, it was so quiet you could have heard a bird chirp.

And then he knocked it in. Just like he said he would. For his fifth straight birdie.

True to Nicklaus' word, the crowd went absolutely bonkers and a deafening roar went up. It was the loudest ovation I've ever heard. You'd have thought everybody around the green had hit the Ohio state lottery at the same moment. Jack was holding up his hands to try to get them to be quiet, and he was probably thinking about me, *You dumb shit, I told you to putt. Now you've got no chance to make par.*

Actually, that was what I was thinking about myself because it was absolute bedlam, and I still had this testy little uphill four-footer while everybody was high-fiving and hand-jiving and uttering orgasmic screams. I half-expected the crowd to start doing the Wave.

I remember looking over at my caddy Mike, because I wanted him to read the putt for me, and he was holding the pin and staring up at the crowd in disbelief. I yelled "Mike . . . Mike . . . MIKE!" at the top of my lungs, and although he was only 20 feet from me, he didn't come close to hearing me. I should mention that Mike Cowan is a card-carrying Deadhead, a guy who never misses a Grateful Dead concert if they're in the area, so he's no stranger to bedlam. But this was overwhelming even to him.

After a few seconds of futility, I had to walk over and touch his shoulder to bring him back to reality. I said, "Mike, read this putt for me," and he gave me a dazed look as if he'd just seen an alien spacecraft land in the bunker. So I finally said, "I got it," and went over to hit the putt.

I took a deep breath and gathered myself, determined to

deal positively with this situation that I had created. When I hit the putt, there was still so much commotion that I never heard the click of the putter on the ball. That's an eerie feeling, almost as though you've whiffed it. But somehow it went in.

I felt really good that I'd been able to make it, and I immediately looked over at Mike and expected him to say, good putt, or way to go, but he was still staring off into the crowd. He looked like Robert DeNiro in the opening scenes of *Awakenings*.

I was finally able to bring Mike back to earth as we walked to the next tee, and he was blown away to hear Nicklaus' remark, how he'd said *"when* I make it."

On the 15th hole, an uphill par-five, Nicklaus poured some adrenaline into his drive, and reached the green with a beautiful one-iron that stopped about 20 feet from the hole. At that point, I thought, this guy's gonna shoot 27 on this nine. As he stood over the eagle putt, Jack knew he was going to make it, and Andy knew he was going to make it, and I knew he was going to make it, and 10,000 misty-eyed Nicklausites knew he was going to make it.

And the ball rolled perfectly up to the cup, peeked in . . . and just tickled around the edge of the hole. I swear that ball saw more lip than Bianca Jagger on her wedding night. But the kiss never came.

Jack had given it his patented victory step, with the putter raised in his left arm, just like he'd done the previous month at Augusta. But this time the golfing gods said, "No, you've reached your limit, Big Fella. It's time to throw a few back."

When it didn't drop, Jack raised his arms in disbelief and covered his head and stared back at the ball, as if to say, Don't you know who I am?

But the ball didn't. It just sat there staring at him with its dimples twinkling in the afternoon sun.

Although it was Jack's sixth birdie in a row, I could sense that he was oddly deflated as he went to the 16th hole. He'd wanted the eagle and he'd hit a perfect putt. When it hadn't dropped, the spell was broken. And what happened to him on the next three holes was as surprising as the previous six. He bogied them all.

As much as he'd used positive thinking to roll to those six birdies, so the negative effect of that near-miss had turned to dust at the end. And it made me appreciate once again how fickle golf can be.

Even though Jack didn't win the tournament, and didn't close out a fabulous round the way he could have, it was nevertheless the most interesting nine holes of golf I've ever watched. I still distinctly remember every shot he hit. And that's because I knew that, at least for a few short hours, I was seeing the best that ever was playing as good as he could. And that's something.

While Nicklaus' run at Muirfield Village is the best stretch of holes I've seen, there have been hundreds of fabulous shots over the years.

One year I watched Jerry Pate make a hole-in-one on the infamous 16th at Cypress Point in the Bing Crosby Pro-Am. It's the only time a pro has ever aced that hole in the tournament, and he did it with an orange golf ball— which I'm sure caused the Scottish shepherds who invented this game to spin like pinwheels in their graves.

The wind was slightly behind us and blowing from right to left, so Jerry hit a one-iron and started it out over the ocean and the cliffs, which takes some guts. But Jerry was having a bad day, and was missing the cut, so it wasn't *that* heroic. Anyway, the ball blew back perfectly, took a nice bounce, and the roll was pure radar.

My trusty partner Jack Lemmon turned to Jerry and said, "If you give me four shots on this hole, I'll play you for a beer." Pate accepted the bet.

As I recall, they tied.

Another great shot I saw firsthand came from Bob Gilder on the final hole in the third round at Westchester in 1982. As a national television audience looked on, Gilder hit a perfect three-wood from 251 yards and holed it for double-eagle. That shot had far greater significance than Pate's, because Gilder had a three-shot lead at the time, and the albatross gave him a nearly insurmountable six-shot lead over Tom Kite, and eight over me. And both of us were paired with him at the time.

The shot also gave Bob a 54-hole total of 192, 18 under par, and a legitimate opportunity to break Mike Souchak's all-time 72-hole Tour record of 257.

I remember I had shot 68 in the opening round of that tournament, but as the scoring was extremely low, I was in about twentieth place. After Jan looked at the scores, she said, "Honey, if you shoot under 65 tomorrow, I'll do something really special for you tomorrow night." It obviously provided serious incentive, because on Friday I shot a course-record 62.

Even with a 10-under par total of 130, I was still three back of Gilder, who'd opened with 64–63. And I'd fallen even further behind as we played the 18th on Saturday. Creamy Carolen, Palmer's one-time caddy, was packing for Bob that day, and when Gilder ripped that three-wood at 18, I said to Creamy, "That's going in."

Bob has a habit of rocking back on his right foot after he's made a big swing, and immediately after he hit it, I remember he rocked back, then took off like a hunting dog after a downed pheasant. Because the green is elevated, we didn't see it go in, but the gallery's reaction was unmistakable. When a shot like that heads for the green, you always look to the gallery to find out how good it is. If there's a huge scream and everybody's arms go up, signaling a touchdown, you know you've holed it. But if their arms go up, then quickly come down, followed by a groan, you have to settle for the field goal.

In this instance, we also had a CBS cameraman there, and he quickly turned to Bob and said, "It's in!"

And Bob was incredulous. He said, "It's in?"

And the cameraman said, "Yes, dammit, it's in!"

Then Gilder asked him one more time, just to make sure.

Jan had walked ahead of us up to the green, and she hadn't seen who'd hit the shot, so she turned to a man next to her and said, "Who hit that?" And he said, "The kid from Oregon."

She started to celebrate until she learned it was the other kid from Oregon, namely Bob Gilder from Corvallis. But that was okay, too, because how often do you see *anyone* make a double-eagle? Gilder went on to win the tournament easily, and Kite and I tied for second. All in all, it was a good week for me, especially my reward on Friday night for the 62.

I've been asked a few times to describe the greatest shot of my life, and that's a tough one. Maybe it was the first time I hit a ball on the face and told my dad, "Hey, this is fun." Or maybe it was the downhill three-iron from 250 yards that I hit onto the green in 1990 to win the Bob Hope Chrysler Classic. But in terms of sheer importance, a fairway bunker shot I hit in Brownsville, Texas, in 1976, has to rank at the top. As usual, a little background is in order.

I turned pro in the fall of 1976, just after my collegiate career had ended. I was engaged to be married to Jan Davis later that year, and so I spent that summer and fall playing as much competition as I could. My goal was to enter the PGA Tour qualifying tournament in Texas in the late fall.

I played in the Western Amateur and the U.S. Amateur that summer, and did fairly well. Then in my last tournament as an amateur, I won the Oregon Open. I shot 65 the last round to beat Bob Duden, a golfer who's a legend in the Pacific Northwest. Duden had won every important tournament in the region about five times, so that was a real confidence-builder. The next week, I went to the Northern California Open at Lake Shastina, and in my professional debut, I won again. First prize was $3,500, and I was so thrilled with the idea of all that money that I thought I could retire and move to Florida on it. I still have the oversized check they presented me at the awards ceremony.

More importantly, I proved to myself that I could play for money without letting the pressure get to me. Then I spent the next month playing in a four-event mini-tour series in Arizona, from which I picked up another fifteen to twenty thousand.

I was on a pretty good roll, but past credentials don't mean a thing at the Tour qualifier. The list is long of great players who've failed that school at least once.

Back then, they had two qualifying tournaments a year, and the fall qualifier was held in Brownsville. There were no regional qualifiers, so basically anybody who could pony up the entry fee could tee it up. That year there were 349 players going after 29 cards, meaning only one in twelve would earn the right to join the Tour. We played six rounds, 108 holes, and it was the most terrifying week

I've ever spent. The only part of my body that stayed loose was my bowels.

You just can't imagine the pressure and fear you feel during that tournament. It's far worse than the Masters or U.S. Open, because in those events you know you've earned your way in, and there's always next week if you don't play well. But if you blow the Tour qualifier, you start practicing lines for your next job, such as, "Would you like paper or plastic, sir?" or "Those wiper blades look a little worn."

I had the additional incentive of knowing that I could sign with the best management group in the world, IMG, if I earned my card. Hughes Norton, who runs IMG's golf division, had already signed Curtis Strange, and he had an interest in me as well, contingent on my making it.

The weather didn't ease the situation any. It was 40 degrees, rainy, and cold. The windchill was right around freezing. A lot of guys wore the kind of ski masks that cover the entire face, with holes just for the eyes and mouth. It looked more like the World Wrestling Federation out there than a golf tournament. I wouldn't have been surprised if the clubhouse leader was Honky Tonk Man, with Jesse "The Body" Ventura two shots back.

Plus, there were none of the other familiar trappings I expected to see at an event that would determine my future: like leaderboards and concession stands. And like fans. Even the ducks had split.

Making matters worse was that I spent the entire week hovering right around the cutoff line. I shot 73s and 74s the first three rounds, 69 in the fourth, and a disappointing 77 in the fifth round. Going into the last day, I needed to shoot even-par or one-over to make it. And the weather was the worst it had been all week. The odds were not in my favor.

I kept grinding, however, making one tough par after another, and as I walked to the final hole, I was informed I needed a par to earn my card. That was less than comforting, because the 18th was a difficult par-four dogleg left, with water guarding the left side of the fairway and the front of the green. Not surprisingly, I blocked my drive right, into a fairway bunker. When I got to the ball, it was not pretty. There were several puddles in the bunker, and although my ball was not in one, I couldn't tell just how soft the sand was. It was sort of like hitting out of freshly mixed cement. My yardage, incidentally, was 180 to the front of the green, with 170 to clear the water.

It was pretty elementary: all I had to do was pick the ball clean, yet hit it high enough to clear the lip of the bunker and the greenside water hazard. Plus, there was wind and rain in my face. I remember thinking, I don't have this shot. And yet I *had* to have this shot or I would not be allowed to wear cranberry Sans-a-Belt slacks for a living.

It even occurred to me that if I didn't par that hole, Jan might head on down the road with one of the guys who'd earned his card, quite possibly Jesse "The Body."

I was so cold and wet and scared walking into the bunker to hit that shot that I thought I might faint. If I'd been playing pinochle, I definitely would have passed. My last thought before taking the club back was to try to hit it thin. And I did.

At that point, God took over and guided that skinny little four-iron shot up onto the green 8 feet from the cup. And I two-putted for par, but not until I'd clogged three more arteries by knocking the first putt four feet past.

Just as I thought, I made it right on the number. My friends Keith Fergus and Mike Sullivan finished first and second. Tied with me were several other players who've gone on to have fine careers on the Tour, including Jay

Haas, Mike Reid, and Don Pooley. Today we still talk about surviving the Nightmare in Brownsville.

One stroke back, and out of luck until the next spring, were my good friends Phil Hancock and Curtis Strange. As it turned out, Hancock won the next qualifier, and Curtis, well, I guess everyone knows things turned out okay for him, too.

CHAPTER 3

Mind Games and Other Matters

ONE OF THE HARDEST QUESTIONS the media can ask a touring professional when he's on a roll is, "Why are you playing so well?"

It's a stumper for many reasons, the main one being that you really don't like to think about it too much, for fear of analyzing away all those good thoughts. Also, when a player has found a secret to lower scoring, he's not about to give it away in an interview. Usually it's a key that works only for him, and to share it is to diminish it.

The typical answer that comes from a Fred Couples or a Davis Love III, or anyone who is shooting the lights out is, "Well, I have a lot of confidence right now." Or, "I feel comfortable over the ball." Or, "Gee, I'm just having a lot of fun these days."

Those are honest answers, although they're not exactly brimming with insight. The guy listening at home is probably thinking, damned right, it's fun to shoot 65 or 66 and take home six-figure checks. Tell me something I don't already know.

But the players aren't necessarily being elusive when they give those simple answers; they're just being honest. We play our best golf when our brain is not working overtime, and our muscles react most effectively when not under great tension. Often, it's easier to play well in the lead of a tournament because you've made a lot of great shots and your confidence is high. When you're trying to fight out of a slump or birdie the last hole to make a cut, the feeling is much different. In the first instance, the stress is positive; in the second, with all those demons of fear screaming warnings at you, the stress can be very negative.

When I didn't play well during parts of 1991 and 1992, it had a lot to do with too much tinkering with my golf swing and overloading the circuitry in my brain.

I've often been criticized for spreading myself too thin, and having too many outside interests away from competitive golf. But that criticism comes from people who don't know me. The truth is, I've played my best golf when I've had the most stuff going on. During stretches of time when I don't have a jam-packed schedule, I get sort of lethargic and don't do as well.

My on-course problems the last two years (apart from the allergies I was suffering) were related to too much instruction. It started when I made some swing changes to accommodate problems I'd had for years with my back. I wanted to use the big muscles more in my golf swing and take the strain off my lower back, and I did that successfully with the help of instructors Jimmy Ballard, John Rhodes, and Randy Henry. But I never quit tinkering, and I was probably guilty of soliciting too much advice from too many different people.

There comes a time when a golf instructor has to look in a student's eye and say, "You're done." The best instruction is like getting a haircut. You sit in the chair, the barber snips away, and after about a half hour he says, "All right, thank you, give me twelve bucks." He's finished, and you go away and don't come back again for two months.

There's a tendency among golf instructors to fall into a "We're never done" attitude. Often, I didn't have enough time to incorporate a lesson into my game before I was trying something else. And I have to blame myself for that. My instructors were only trying to help. So in 1992, I started "de-toxing," if you will, from golf lessons. I got confused, so I had to clean out the circuitry from an overload of information. I found that Fred Couples' swing was a good model, but I'll get to that later.

Jackie Burke told me a story once that applies to my situation last year. A friend of Jackie's had a wonderful wooden statue of a dog in his office. Jackie raved about the statue and asked him where he had gotten it. The friend said, "Well, thanks. I carved it myself."

Burke said, "Wow! That's incredible. How did you do that?"

And the friend said, "I just cut away everything that didn't look like a dog."

That's a good way of looking at golf instruction, and even golf course architecture. In designing a golf course, you just cut away and move dirt and remove everything that doesn't look like a golf course, and in golf instruction the teacher eventually has to say, "Enough cutting, now go play."

Unfortunately, I kept whittling away at the foundation of my swing until there was hardly any shape or artistry left . . . just an ugly lump of wood. What had once looked like a dog had been whittled down to a rat. So I went back to my natural swing, and any inherent athletic ability I might have, and reestablished confidence from there.

Golf swings are like snowflakes: there are no two exactly alike. I try to emphasize how different they all are when I do my swing impersonations. When I do Lee Trevino, I line up way open, take the club back way outside, and drop it back to the inside. When I do Miller Barber, I make sure that the first thing that comes back is my right elbow, which flies out as far away from my body as I can get it. When I do Johnny Miller, I try to do an early set and cock the club as much as I can. These swings are as different from one another as they can be, but they belong to players who have all been tremendously successful on Tour. The point is, they all return to the impact zone in the same position.

When you're playing your best golf, you're not aware of these idiosyncrasies. You just put your hands on the club, take it back, hit the ball, and go find it. The sole aim is to get it into the hole, and even though it appears the golf hole gets bigger as you approach it, it's really an optical illusion, because the ball fits as easily into the hole from 180 yards as it does from two inches. You just have to understand that and get the ball and the mind moving in that direction.

Sometimes we get so stuck on fundamental and technical thoughts that we forget that the golf ball is simply meant to be projected in a certain direction toward a flag stuck in a hole in the ground.

And here's where Couples comes in. His success in 1991 and 1992 really changed my outlook on the golf swing. As I said, I had gotten too technical with my swing changes, and here was a guy winning everything with a beautiful-looking swing, but one that was far from classic if you

broke it down. Fred would credit his instructors Dick
Harmon and Paul Marchand for preserving his natural
ability and working within it. They've never made Fred
start from scratch when making a swing adjustment.

After Fred won at Bay Hill by nine strokes in early 1992,
there was an action picture of him on the cover of *Golf
World* magazine. His right palm was completely off the golf
club just after impact. The only contact points were the tips
of his thumb and little finger. That told me that poor
Freddie was a slapper. All he did was slap it around in 19
under par that week and kick everybody's butt.

I've done many clinics with Freddie over the last ten
years, and when I ask him to come up and hit some fades,
he'll hit half a dozen of the prettiest fades you've ever seen.
So for the benefit of the crowd, I'll ask him what he does
when he needs to hit a fade. And he always looks at me
with that infectious grin and says, "Gee, Peter, I don't
know. I just get up to the ball and I see it start down the
left side of the fairway and kind of slice back to the right,
and when I have that picture in my mind I make my
swing."

Everybody in the grandstand always laughs. So I ask him
to hit some hooks, and he'll hit half a dozen great-looking
right-to-left shots, and when he tries to explain he blushes
and says, "I really don't know. I just get up there and see
the ball hooking and then make the swing, and the ball
hooks."

What Fred is describing is a sort of Zen-like state, which
Ben Hogan called "muscle memory," and it's the essence
of the teachings of my friend Chuck Hogan (no relation).
That is, using your mind to direct your golf shots. In
Freddie, it comes across at times as lackadaisical, carefree,
and non-analytical, but what he's really tapped into is the
essence of great golf, which is arriving at a zone of total

relaxation and total confidence. He just steps up to the golf ball, takes a deep breath to relax, takes it back, and whomps it. Then he goes and finds it and whomps it again. And when he adds up the whomps, the total is usually lower than that of the other 143 whompers.

Couples' casual, wonderfully fun approach caused me to realize that I was thinking too much about where the clubhead was halfway into my backswing, and where it was on the follow-through. It was almost a "connect-the-dots" exercise. As I've often said, golf is really a mind game; in fact, it is a sport that relies almost entirely on the imagination of the individual playing it. The golf ball is in motion for only about six minutes in a four-hour round of golf played in even-par. So that means that the other three hours and fifty-four minutes are spent either reflecting on the last shot or imagining what might happen on the next one.

As Shivas Irons says, "It's all in the walking, lad."

That's just another intriguing aspect that makes this sport so wonderful. Ninety-eight percent of golf is played between the ears. I didn't really appreciate this until I got to know Chuck Hogan and believe in him as a great golf educator. I had known Chuck only casually as a golf pro in Oregon, when I received a couple of letters from him suggesting that we get together. He felt he could give me some help with the mental side of the game. In the summer of 1984, suffering from both physical and mental wounds (a bad back and low confidence), I drove down to Eugene, Oregon, where I'd gone to college, and spent four days with Chuck. He was gaining a good reputation, and I certainly needed help.

We had several long conversations before we started doing any drills. During one of our talks, he held his fingers about two inches apart and said, "See this ball?"

"What ball?" I said, darned certain he was holding nothing but air.

"Don't you see a ball in my hand?" he said.

"Am I supposed to?"

"Yes," he said.

"Okay, I do," I conceded, although, of course, I didn't.

"Take this ball from my hand, and we're going to go to the back putting green at Eugene Country Club and practice making putts with it," Chuck said.

Now this made me a little squeamish, because having played Eugene C.C. as my home course in college, and having been on the Tour several years, most of the members at the club knew who I was. But part of Chuck's theory is that the best ego is no ego, so this would be part of the exercise.

When we got there, Chuck told me to drop the "ball" about ten feet from the hole and try to knock it in. I looked up on the veranda overlooking the practice green, and several people waved and the rest looked on intently.

I started to line up the "putt," and then I backed off.

"This is kind of embarrassing," I said. "They're watching me putt without a ball."

"What do you care, as long as they all go in?" Chuck said.

So I hit the first putt, and he said, "Where did it go?"

I said, "I made it."

And he said, "Good. Because if you'd have missed it, your mental problems would be too deep for me to solve."

I had a good laugh at that, and kept putting. I'd stroke the putt, my eyes would follow it down the line and watch it go into the hole. Then I'd lift the miniature flag out and dump the ball to the side, rake it back a few feet, and putt again.

Sure enough, I kept holing one imaginary putt after

another, and started to get mesmerized with the whole process. After I'd hit fifteen or twenty putts, I noticed a man sitting on the veranda, intently watching me and eating lunch at the same time. He was obviously more fascinated with my practice technique than his lunch, because he had mayonnaise all over his mouth and chin.

"Look at that guy," I said to Chuck, under my breath. "I've knocked ten putts in the middle of the hole with an invisible ball, and that guy is only one-for-four hitting his mouth with a turkey croissant."

Despite my perplexed gallery, I stayed on the practice green for forty minutes and fulfilled my goal of making every single putt I hit. Obviously, I had also learned to put my ego aside, at least for a time.

In the next few days, Chuck worked with me on many concepts and taught me that we have the answers to our questions deep inside—that it's just a matter of listening to ourselves. He also emphasized that our subconscious mind didn't know the difference between real and imagined, so if we trained our imagination to do positive things, such as consistently making ten-foot putts, we could make real ten-foot putts as well.

The entire week I was home I never hit a real golf ball; I just worked on mental exercises. When I went to the next tournament on the schedule, the Colonial National Invitational in Fort Worth, I was very relaxed, and concerned only with practicing what I'd learned.

What do you know? I won the tournament, beating Payne Stewart with a birdie on the first hole of sudden death. That victory was extra special for another reason. My father had undergone his initial cancer surgery back in Portland, and I was able to dedicate the victory to him. It made both of us feel pretty darned good.

Needless to say, I became a true believer in the theories

of Chuck Hogan, and am to this day. Whenever my mind gets cluttered with too many thoughts, I visit Chuck and he really helps me clear my head.

On one occasion I asked Chuck to work with Jack Lemmon prior to our annual appearance in the AT&T National Pro-Am. Jack gets very uptight on the golf course, so Chuck tried an exercise to take him out of the reality of the situation.

"Jack, you're the greatest actor in the world," Chuck told him, "and your role in the movie you're about to star in is to play a man competing in a national pro-am, who rises to the occasion and plays brilliant golf, topped off by holing a putt on the final green to win the tournament."

A little smile came over Jack's face, and he said, "Hey, I like that idea."

Well, I wish I could tell you this session worked as well as mine had, but at least for 27 holes the concept took hold, and Jack played very well. After a while, however, the pressure of the tournament and all the distractions snapped my partner out of that zone, and we missed the cut again. As Chuck put it: "Unfortunately, Jack ended up playing the role of an anchor rather than a Kite."

Hey, if I could successfully apply Chuck's method every time, I'd have won four Grand Slams by now.

Another minefield I've learned to handle in my career is an affliction known as rabbit ears. It's caused by letting peoples' off-the-cuff comments slip through your auditory canal and into your brain. It's especially prevalent with golf broadcasters.

One occurrence in 1982 really got to me. CBS announcer Ben Wright was at his post on the 17th hole at the Westchester Classic. I was having a good tournament, in second behind Gilder during Saturday's play, and I'd placed in the top three at Memorial and Atlanta in recent weeks. So I was on a pretty good roll.

CBS flashed a graphic on the screen that indicated I had hit an incredible percentage of greens in regulation in recent weeks, something like 63 out of 72 at Memorial and 64 of 72 at Atlanta, and that I'd missed only two greens out of 52 by the time I reached Ben's hole on Saturday. It was actually just one of these streaks one goes through—even my bad shots were still catching the corner of the green. Johnny Miller has said that the surest sign you're playing well is when your bad shots aren't that bad. That was the case for me then. My bad shots were still finding the putting surface, but Ben didn't read it that way.

He said, on camera, "Wow, this kid can't putt. Look how many greens he's hit." And then he said to Ken Venturi, in the booth at 18, "Kenny, can you give Peter a putting lesson? He looks like a good young player, but he needs to learn how to putt."

Well, I went on to tie for second with Tom Kite at 14 under par behind Gilder.

When I watched the replay of Westchester and heard Ben's comment, it hurt me, because I thought I was a pretty good putter. I'd been knocking on the door of victory several times in recent weeks, but nobody was home. Or maybe someone was inside but the door was jammed. Anyway, that started a period in which the "conventional wisdom" (a misnomer if there ever was one) was that I was a good ball-striker but a poor putter. And it caused my self-image to suffer with the short stick.

I got back at Ben when I did an interview with *Sports Illustrated* a couple years later, and relayed the anecdote to writer Jaime Diaz. I explained to Jaime that one of Chuck Hogan's theories was to dispel negative thoughts from your head by plotting ways to make them disappear. Jaime came up with the idea of staging a photograph in which we airlifted a Ben Wright dummy out of the CBS booth by helicopter. Ben and I both laugh about the incident now, and I've learned not to be so sensitive to stupid commentary.

Another instance of rabbit ears occurred just a few days after I'd won the Sammy Davis Jr.–Greater Hartford Open in 1984. Hartford had been just one more great week in a really fun year for me, coming on top of the win at Colonial and that great week in the British Open at St. Andrews. Everything Chuck Hogan had preached to me had really sunk in.

Hogan had also espoused that at the level of the PGA Tour, a player has proven many times over that his swing is reliable under pressure, and that the biggest window of improvement is in the mystical side of golf. Basically, Chuck convinced me that I didn't need to be such a perfectionist about my golf swing, and that I had to play more by feel. And that's what I was doing that summer. I had "felt" my way to a solid victory at Hartford, and a couple days later was home in Portland watching the replay of the final round. I was hitting a seven-iron to the 14th green, a shot that landed in the middle of the green, and Steve Melnyk, who was doing the commentary for CBS, had made a comment about my backswing.

He said something to the effect that Peter Jacobsen makes kind of an awkward-looking backswing, he takes the club and lays it off quite a bit, so that the club points way to the left of the target, but he somehow gets it through the hitting area and the ball goes straight.

Now I understand that commentators love to play the

role of analyst, but the Golf Hall of Fame is full of players with unusual-looking swings, and some of the prettiest swings you've ever seen in your life are made on the far end of the public driving range by guys who couldn't break an egg with a baseball bat.

Anyway, that comment really affected my ego and buried itself in my subconscious. I let Steve know about it when I next saw him. I was hitting balls with Lee Trevino on the driving range at the World Series of Golf, and when Steve walked over I got it off my chest. I told him that I didn't appreciate his criticizing my swing at Hartford and that it didn't make him look too smart, seeing as I was hitting every green and winning the tournament.

Although I went on to finish third that week at the World Series, I still couldn't get the notion out of my head that I had a flawed swing, and that I had to fix it so a broadcaster couldn't criticize it on national television. My rabbit ears had infected my brain, and as a result I didn't play well the remainder of that year. Through my own hypersensitivity, I had fallen out of playing by feel and into a stupid search for the perfect swing.

In my own stints working as a broadcaster, I never criticize a player's swing, because although I realize the television golf audience is hungry for instruction, analyzing swings can only show that there are a thousand different methods for hitting a shot well. Fred Couples' right hand sometimes comes off the club. Any club pro would scold you soundly for that. Jack Nicklaus has a flying right elbow. That's also bad. Walter Hagen made a big lunge at the ball. Purists would cringe at videos of his swing.

I guess I shouldn't have felt too bad laying off the club at the top of my backswing in the middle of my best season on the Tour. But it certainly wasn't Melnyk's fault. All I really needed to prolong my good play was a set of earplugs. But that's what the Tour is all about—learning from experience.

While I still have Fred Couples on my mind, I should mention that his recent status as one of the best players in the world has been great for golf. I've known Fred since he was about nineteen and playing at the University of Houston. He grew up in Seattle, and players from the Pacific Northwest have a mutual admiration society because there aren't many of us on Tour.

But more than that, Freddie is the type of player who improves the image of the sport because he's a kind person, has no arrogance, and is totally focused on golf. I don't think his playing career will be the slightest bit diminished by outside interests, because for him golf is the biggest turn-on. He's also not swayed by the money, because he's made a ton of it over the last ten years and he's hung on to most of it.

When Fred won the Masters in 1992, which completed an incredible run where he'd finished in the top six in twenty of his previous twenty-five tournaments, he put a stop to a lot of the talk about European domination of professional golf. Couples had led the American Ryder Cup team to victory over the Europeans in 1991 and had stopped a four-year run of European winners at Augusta.

Remember, one of the reasons the Americans stopped dominating golf and fell off the ladder a bit was because of the responsibilities that come with corporate contracts, endorsements, media pressure, and the responsibilities that players feel to "do the right thing."

It's extremely difficult to turn down the offers that come when you've reached the pinnacle of golf. Look at players like Curtis Strange, Greg Norman, and Payne Stewart.

They're offered incredible sums of money to sponsor products or compete overseas, and it's a chance for them to provide permanent financial security for their families.

If you have an opportunity to take a $150,000 offer to go overseas, or to sign a five-million-dollar contract to wear a brand of clothing or play a certain make of golf club, your better judgment tells you to take it. If you turn it down, you have to live with that voice inside you that says, "You could start hitting snap hooks tomorrow, or shanking your chip shots, or you might get the yips. Take the money while you can."

Remember, there are no guaranteed contracts or injured-reserve lists on the PGA Tour, so relatively short reigns at the top of the world are common. Nick Faldo has enjoyed a longer stint at the top because he has maintained an incredible focus on his golf. As other sports champions have said, "It's tougher staying at number one than it was getting there."

It just makes me appreciate all the more those special golfers like Hogan, Palmer, Nicklaus, and Watson, who were able to stay on top for long stretches of time. I could write a whole chapter about Arnold Palmer. In fact, I think I will.

CHAPTER 4

Arnold Palmer

I CAME BY my admiration for Arnold Palmer naturally: I inherited it from my dad. Dad was an excellent player in his prime—a legitimate scratch golfer—and he always joked that his handicap increased as his number of dependents rose. He went from a zero to a one after David was born, to a two after me, a three after Paul, and a four after Susie. Fortunately, the same progression never occurred to me or I'd have had to find a real job soon after our first child Amy was born.

Anyway, like so many golfers in the 1960s, Palmer and Nicklaus were Dad's two heroes, and, of course, they were on television all the time, because one or the other was winning every week. Nicklaus was always in control—cool, collected, and obviously special—but Palmer was the one that really caught my attention, because he was unique. He combined grace, force, and brute strength in an unnatural motion that seemed perfectly suited to his personality.

He'd take that furious swing, and when he got to impact

he seemed to be on the toes of his shoes, his feet spinning, his heels coming off the ground, and the club going in fifteen different directions. Depending on how many hazards the ball had to elude, that's exactly how many neck jerks and head tilts he employed. He looked like a guy trying to dodge hornets.

Even as a kid, I thought: what an incredible swing this guy has! The ball had left the clubface and yet here he was twisting and jerking and urging it on down the fairway, and the gallery would go nuts, and Palmer would snatch up his tee and hike up his trousers and off he'd go to rip an iron right at the flag.

So I started practicing his swing, and that became my first impression: doing Arnold Palmer in the backyard. I was all of ten years old. It's a shame *Star Search* wasn't on the air back then. I would have gotten three and a half stars in the Junior Swing Impersonation competition and gotten to meet the Junior Spokesmodel.

I'll always remember how I first met him. It was around a dozen years later, in my rookie year of 1977. Coincidentally, it occurred at a tournament that has become very special to me through the years, the Bing Crosby Pro-Am. We had the Monday qualifying system back then, and I had missed the first two qualifiers at Phoenix and Tucson. I had finally made it into my first official PGA Tour event at the Crosby and was out playing a practice round at Monterey Peninsula Country Club, one of the courses used in the rotation at the time.

It was late Tuesday afternoon before the tournament, and I had played the front nine and was somewhere on the back side when I noticed a large cloud of dust billowing up in the distance. It was like in the old cowboy movies when there's a cattle drive or the posse's ridin' up on the bad guys, and I knew something important was happening. But I went about my business and, sensing I didn't have time to finish all 18 holes, I cut over to the 16th tee.

As this was my first time on the course, I really didn't know the layout of the holes. I just knew I had about half an hour of sunlight left. So I hit a couple drives off the 16th, when all of a sudden, out of nowhere, an incredible throng of spectators emerged over the rise behind me and surrounded the back of the tee.

It was like when the entire Bolivian army encircled Butch Cassidy and the Sundance Kid and aimed their rifles at them. These people weren't armed and dangerous, but they were sure looking at me with expressions that said: Who is this kid, and what's he doing out here?

And then the Red Sea parted, and who should walk through it but Arnold Palmer himself. The King. He couldn't have been more regal had he been wearing a robe and carrying a staff.

I felt a chill come over me. I was shocked and embarrassed. I mean, here was my boyhood idol, and I'd just cut right in front of him, and hit two balls no less. I wanted to crawl into the ball-washer and disappear. But true to his character, Palmer walked up to me, shook my hand, introduced himself, and said, "How are you?"

I managed to squeak out a "fine," although I wasn't. And he said, "Could we join you?"

Now that was the first thing he ever said to me, and it struck me so funny because I was thinking, "Can *you* join *me?*" What I wanted to say was, "Can I have your permission to crawl under a rock and stay there for a day as penance for getting in your way?"

But, of course, I acted cool, considered his request for a long second, and said, "Sure, love to have you," like it was no big deal.

This was gut-check time, even if there was no money on the line, because in addition to meeting my idol for the first time, I also met Mark McCormack, who was Palmer's amateur partner. McCormack was head of IMG, with whom I had signed just a few weeks before, but I wasn't sure he even knew who I was.

Nevertheless, I was determined not to let the situation intimidate me, or worry about embarrassing myself. I've always loved the challenge of golf, whatever it may be, so I looked on this as just another challenge, and a darned good preparation for the coming week. After all, this was just a practice round, so I couldn't worry about future endorsements, or impressing these guys. My goal at that point in my career was simple survival. All I wanted to do was make some cuts, make some money, and keep my playing privileges. I was recently married and I wanted to be able to make it to that Christmas and have enough money to buy my wife a nice present.

But back to the 16th hole. Arnold hit a nice drive, and I remember feeling good that both of my drives were past his. If I felt a moment of cockiness, however, it quickly evaporated when I snap-hooked a seven-iron into the bunker. Fortunately, I got it up and down, and that eased my nerves. On the next tee, Arnold asked me what kind of ball I was playing, and I told him it was a Titleist.

He said, "You ought to try one of these *good* balls," and tossed me a Palmer ball. I hit it and liked it, so he tossed me a three-pack and said, "As a rookie starting out, you need good equipment, and these might help you along the way." He was sincerely trying to be helpful, because it wasn't as if he needed the endorsement of an unknown kid from Oregon playing his golf balls.

As abruptly as the experience of playing golf with Arnold Palmer had begun, so it ended. After holing out at 18, Palmer thanked me, wished me luck in my career, and disappeared into the madding crowd. When I looked up a few seconds after shaking his hand, everyone was gone. I mean *everyone*. There was no more Arnie's Army, only Peter's Poltergeists. I had to shake my head to make certain it had really happened.

When Mike Stoll and I conceived The Fred Meyer Challenge in 1985, we agreed that if we were going to have a successful tournament, we needed to start with Palmer and build a field from there. Early in 1986, at the Bob Hope Chrysler Classic in Palm Springs, I called Arnold and told him we were starting a new tournament in Portland to bring world-class golf back to the Pacific Northwest, and that we'd really be honored to have him play. Without hesitation, he said, "Sure, Peter. I'd love to help you out."

When I put down the phone, we knew right then we had launched a tournament. For the last five years in a row, I've taken Arnold as my partner in the Challenge because I can have no bigger honor as a golfer than to be partners with the man who's done so much for golf.

We've had some wonderful tournaments together, as well. We've finished third twice in the Fred Meyer, but our shining moment together was in the 1990 Shark Shootout, hosted by Greg Norman. In that tournament, Fred Couples and Raymond Floyd shot 34 under par for three rounds, with an incredible 57 in the alternate-shot segment the second day, and they lapped the field. But

Arnold and I finished second, three strokes ahead of the next three teams.

The first round that year, Curtis Strange and Mark O'Meara shot a best-ball 59, with Curtis making 11 birdies on his own. Meanwhile, my partner was struggling at the start. Palmer hit a bad drive on the first hole, another bad one on the second, and sort of a pop-up on the fourth, but I was able to birdie two of those holes. Arnold came over to me on the fifth tee and said, "Son of a bitch, I'm just not *hitting* that ball."

Because I love to needle him, I said, "Don't worry, partner. I'll carry you, just like I do every year in this thing."

Now it's been said of Palmer that he doesn't walk onto the tee of a golf hole. Rather he climbs into it, almost as though it were a boxing ring. And that's the way he looked right then, like he was ready to toss some leather around. He gave me a double-take, as if he were not certain whether I was kidding or not, and then stood up on number five, pumped his drive past everybody in the group, hit a three-wood into a greenside bunker, then holed his sand shot for an eagle. He had enough fire in his eyes to roast a pig. We went on to shoot 61 (which, incidentally, was his age at the time), then the last day shot 60. It was so great to see him turn it on, just like he'd done on television when I was a kid.

We also had the low round at the Fred Meyer Challenge last year when we shot a 63 at the Oregon Golf Club on the final day. A couple of times that week, Arnold got big laughs from the crowd. We had a poor start the first day, bogeying three of the first eight holes, and although we salvaged the round with some late birdies, at one point on the back nine I said to Arnold, "Partner, we may not win this year, but we'll get 'em next year."

And he gave me a startled look. "Next year?" he said. "Peter, at my age I don't even buy green bananas."

Also that week, during a clinic on the 18th green in front of the grandstands, I was talking with Billy Andrade, who had attended Wake Forest University on an Arnold Palmer golf scholarship. I asked Billy what the grant included.

With a straight face, he said, "Well, you get tuition, books, food, a car, a plane, and girls." The crowd laughed, and Arnold leaned over and said, "Shoot, I think I'm going back to school."

The truth about Arnold is that he still hits it beautifully from tee to green, but he doesn't believe in his putting the way he should. So much of golf is mental, and Arnold believes he hits it better than ninety percent of the players, but he sometimes doesn't believe the putts will drop.

I always include my impersonation of him when I do exhibitions, and he's seen me do it over and over, and he even joins in if I ask him. I added one part a few years ago that is pure Palmer. I pretend I'm Arnold studying the shot, and I'm hitching my trousers and checking the tops of the trees to judge the wind, but I'm still not sure. So I reach inside my shirt, pull out a few chest hairs and toss them up to check the wind. Everybody laughs, because Palmer's so manly it would almost be in character for him to do something like that. Every now and then, when he's watching me do him, I get just a little uneasy for fear that people think I'm mocking him. But Arnold always laughs, and he understands me perfectly.

I'm often asked by friends what I've learned from Palmer, and the answer is, plenty, and much of it just by paying attention. I like watching Arnold hit practice balls, because he has such a great swing plane. He's good at repeating the same action over and over, and he's so strong through the hitting area. He's also imparted a few pearls of wisdom, on those few occasions when I keep my mouth shut and ears open. Arnold has said to me many times, "Peter, you are only out here to win. Second doesn't matter. Second is about as important as fifty-second. Winning is the reason you are playing."

Now while I haven't won as many tournaments as I'd like, I understand what he's saying, and when he offers me this advice I sometimes rub up against him, in the hope that a little of that Palmer magic will rub off on me.

There was a special moment for me in 1991, at Arnold's tournament at Bay Hill. Keeping in mind that most of the players playing today, myself included, had not seen Arnold in his prime, with his hair falling in his face and blood coming out of his fingernails from scratching and scraping his way to a 67 to beat somebody, I decided to thank him in a small way.

Between organizing and hosting the tournament, and even redesigning the course on which it's played, Arnold had not made the cut at Bay Hill in a while, but he did make it in 1991. So after Friday's round, I went to the bakery department of a local supermarket in Orlando and told the woman I needed a sheet cake that would feed 200 people or so. She asked me when I needed it, and I said the next day. She said that would be impossible, that it would take at least four days. I told her it was for Arnold Palmer, and she said I could pick it up in an hour.

I had the Palmer umbrella logo put on it, and the Nestlé Invitational logo and an inscription that read: "Congratulations, Arnold, on making the cut, and thanks for a great week from all the players."

As luck would have it, all seventy-five players who'd made the cut were in the locker room Sunday morning, waiting for a decision on a rain delay, when we presented it to him. You could tell from their faces that they all held him in awe.

I made a little speech and ribbed him about finally making the cut, and he was really touched. He took a moment to gather himself, so I needled him a little more, and then he took the cake knife and pretended that he was going to cut my throat.

So often, with the fast pace of the Tour, we move from week to week, never looking back to thank or show appreciation for the people who made it all possible. That was a chance for a younger generation of professional golfers to thank the man who's probably most responsible of all for the great showcase known as the PGA Tour.

CHAPTER 5

"Impressions" of the Tour

THERE'S A LOT OF PRESSURE playing golf for a living, and if you don't step back from it every now and again your brain will calcify and become crustier than an elephant's toenail.

Laughter is by far the best remedy I've found to deal with stress, so in those relaxed moments around the Tour when I'm with friends in the locker room or on the driving range, I just love to get goofy and start laughing. Laughter is the reason I enjoy impersonating other players' swings, and why the fans get such a kick out of it as well. Who doesn't like to laugh?

Although I had practiced doing impressions at home as a kid, the first guy I saw do them in public was Billy Harmon, one of the many talented sons of the late Masters champion, Claude Harmon. It was at the driving range at Thunderbird CC in Palm Springs when I was fifteen, and he had Gary Player down cold, from the voice to the swing to the tilt of the head. People would just howl when Billy would do his stuff, and I thought right then that mimicry would be a great way to have fun.

Through the years, I played around with it, adding a new player from time to time to my basic repertoire, choosing those with distinctive swings, and whom I really admired. I did them for an audience on the Tour for the first time in 1978, during a long-driving contest in Atlanta. The Tour had its own special competition, and the winners qualified for the National Long Drive contest sponsored by *Golf Digest*.

Although I'm only average long as far as the Tour goes, my buddy D. A. Weibring said I should enter and give the crowd a taste of something different. We were allowed just six shots, so I hit the first three as Peter Jacobsen, the fourth as Arnold Palmer, the fifth as Johnny Miller, and I closed with Hubert Green. I believe that in the "Sybil" derby, Miller won, followed by Jacobsen #2 and Jacobsen #3. Unfortunately, none were long enough to qualify for the real gorilla show at the Nationals, but the crowd didn't care. They just wanted to see more impressions. I couldn't believe the ovation I got.

That's when D.A. and I realized that we could make this dog yodel. Shortly afterward, we started doing junior clinics at the Tour stops, in which we'd offer groups of up to 200 kids some basic golf instruction. Then D.A. would play the straight man as I did impressions.

In exchange for our time, the tournament sponsors would give us courtesy cars (this was in the days before every player received one), or invitations to play in the pro-am. In a couple of instances, we even got exemptions into the tournament, which was pretty juicy for a couple of guys in only their second year on the Tour.

Those youth clinics got so popular that before long we

were doing about twelve to fifteen a year. Several offers also came in to do special outings away from the Tour. One week, D.A. and I traveled around the country and did five outings in a seven-day period. We would do the clinic, the impressions, a question-and-answer session, then play one hole each with every foursome in a pro-am. It was exhausting but a lot of fun.

The outings became a nice sideline, but the best part was that we hopefully turned a lot of boys and girls on to golf and away from some of the other damaging distractions that kids face today. Parents can be pretty certain that their children are not getting into trouble if they're on the golf course, and the kids are playing a game that will help them build character.

I'm really proud of the fact that the clinics D.A. and I did have grown into a full-fledged corporate program for kids. They were originally underwritten by Gatorade and are now sponsored by Coca-Cola. Every week on Tour, boys and girls are offered instruction and inspiration from the top professionals. There's even a club giveaway program, to help kids get started.

Sometime during this period, I got a call from Bob Hope, who asked me to do my impressions at the Bob Hope Chrysler Classic Ball. I told him I had all these props, and that I really wasn't sure I could do it inside, and he just said, "Peter, you'll figure it out."

So I took that to mean we were on the bill, ready or not.

The night of the dinner we were all in tuxedos, and Bob and former President Gerald Ford were the co-emcees. When they announced our act, D.A. went out first and introduced me as Lee Trevino. I was standing in the wings next to these two distinguished Americans, and as I took off my evening jacket and cummerbund and tie, and put on a Mexican hat, I looked for somewhere to put the clothes. Well, there wasn't anywhere, so I shoved them in President Ford's arms, and he politely held it all while I did Trevino. Next, I did Palmer, and then Miller, and each time there was a wardrobe change. Like it or not, the President was stuck with the job. After about four or five changes, Tom Dreesen, a comedian on the bill, came over to me and said, in an alarmed voice, "Peter, Peter, you're treating the former President of the United States like he's a damn stagehand!"

I hurried over to Mr. Ford and took all the stuff out of his arms and dumped it in Bob Hope's lap. The President seemed slighted that I'd replaced him, so he lifted the pile off Bob and said, "I'm holding this stuff, thank you." Apparently, he liked the job.

Dreesen followed our act and shook his head as he took the microphone. "Ladies and gentlemen," he said, "this is a first. I've opened for Frank Sinatra for years, but I've never followed a professional-golfer act doing swing impressions. Especially one that uses a former President as a wardrobe man."

After five or six years, we decided to cut back on our performance schedule. I was becoming known more as the Mimic of the Tour than as Peter Jacobsen, Tour player, and I didn't want a sideshow to overshadow my main purpose for being out there. I knew the only way I could change this image was to become a better player. Lee Trevino is an example of what I mean. Although Lee is one of the funniest, most entertaining personalities in the history of golf, he is known as a champion first, and as a funny guy second. As much as I enjoyed entertaining crowds, I wanted to be more like Arnold Palmer than Rich Little.

The clinics also became very time-consuming, and were

getting in the way of my preparation for the tournaments. I remember a broadcaster once saying on the air, "Peter Jacobsen does such great imitations. He must really work on them. Maybe he should spend more time imitating his own swing."

Although the criticism stung, I knew that if I didn't prove myself first as a player, there was a danger of creating a monster that would eat me alive. In the last several years, I've limited my impersonations to about four performances a year. But I still enjoy doing them as much as ever.

Creating impersonations of golfers is no different than a political cartoonist's doing caricatures of Presidents. You choose one or two distinctive features and exaggerate them for effect. When the cartoonists drew Jimmy Carter, it was his smile and teeth. With Reagan, it was the pompadour hair and wrinkled neck. With Bush, the prominent jaw.

I have about ten players who are always in my repertoire, and the impressions have come together from a variety of sources. For my Craig Stadler imitation, I got pointers from his good friend Jeff Miller when we were in Japan for the Dunlop Phoenix tournament. We came up with the idea of pulling the pants way down in back, pouring two buckets of range balls down the front of my shirt, and wearing the facial expression of a man who has just bitten into a bad avocado.

I also worked on the walk. I took that from his nickname. Craig Stadler walks like a walrus would walk . . . if a walrus could walk. His legs never really bend at the knee. All you see moving is this big upper body with a mustache on it.

As the final exclamation point to the Stadler routine, I always drop the club and walk away while the ball is still in flight. I know when I do this skit in front of Craig, he'll laugh harder than anyone in the crowd. That's because he's a great guy who's exactly the opposite of the scowling creature you see shooting all those frustrating 67s and 68s. (Craig's got his own imitation of Seve Ballesteros that is priceless . . . in Spanish, no less.)

After Stadler's controversial disqualification from the Shearson Lehman Brothers Andy Williams Open in San Diego in 1987, I had some fun recreating the incident in which Craig placed a towel on the wet ground and kneeled on it to hit a recovery shot from under a tree. For those who don't remember, he was disqualified the next day when it was ruled that he'd built an artificial stance and hadn't called a two-shot penalty on himself. It ended up costing him $37,000, which was $36,950 more than he paid for the pants.

Perhaps the best-received impersonation I've ever done was with Craig at The Fred Meyer Challenge in 1991. Tom Dreesen, who'd first demonstrated his ad-libbing skill to me at the Bob Hope Classic dinner years before, came up with the idea. We had Stadler come out and hit a few shots for the people in the grandstands. Then Tom announced that he had a big surprise: Craig's long-lost brother "Haig" Stadler had resurfaced after several years away from civilization, and was here to show that he, too, had a little ability as a golfer. So with my pants halfway down my rear, and my shirt bulging with about seventy-five golf balls, I came out and hugged my more famous brother, and then we hit a few balls, using the identical swing. It was truly a touching moment in the annals of golf.

I really have fun doing Johnny Miller, because he has such distinct mannerisms. A key to doing Miller is the walk. He's sort of knock-kneed when he walks, as if he's trying to hold an aspirin between his knees. He also lifts his legs from the inner ankle, which gives the appearance that he's trying to walk through chicken wire without getting his spikes caught. The knees come straight up. Of course, the shirt collar has to be up, and he always has that squinty-eyed look, like he's gazing into the sun. Which is only appropriate for a guy they call the Golden Boy.

Later in his career, Johnny started swinging harder and both his heels would come off the ground at impact. On the follow-through he would roll onto his left ankle so severely that it was almost flattened on the ground when he finished. Of course, after his iron shots landed two feet from the pin, he'd always hold up his index finger, which served a dual purpose: it both thanked the crowd and signaled his position on the leader board.

I've always considered Johnny a role model, both as a golfer and a person. I'd especially like to imitate his twenty-three career victories.

Lanny Wadkins is another guy I love to do. He has a cocky way of carrying himself that lets all the other players know that he's the sheriff. And he is. Lanny's about the last guy on earth you'd want to face in a golf showdown with your life on the line. When I do Lanny, I get a lot of movement going with the head. Then I step up and address it, with my head cocked slightly back. I never take a practice swing, because Lanny's never taken one in his life. They're a waste of time and slow down play. Then I swing as fast as I can, but I don't hold the finish. I bring the club back down to waist-high and start twirling it in my hands. Then I tear off my golf glove and start walking. Fast.

If I were to do Lanny putting, I'd have to have a few teeth pulled and work on my stick-handling, because he hockeys those short putts around the hole. And he's good at it. Try standing on the wrong side of the cup and banging one-footers backwards into the hole if you don't believe me. Lanny converts about 98 percent of 'em.

Tom Kite's got a distinctive style, with that fist pumping

and his head cocked as if to say, "How about that?" As in, How about the fact I've won eight million dollars and continue to beat the crap out of all these guys with so much more God-given talent than me?

With Tom I put on dark glasses and his new-look straw hat, and slather several layers of chapstick over my lips, like a little girl who's just discovered her mother's make-up kit. Early in his career, Tom used to hold his finish until every Kodak on the property could go through six rolls of film. So when I was doing him years ago, I would freeze that finish until it felt like my spine was ready to snap. (I wonder if that's how I developed back problems?)

And then there is Raymond Floyd. He approached me with a big smile on his face after he'd won the U.S. Open in 1986 at Shinnecock Hills.

"Am I good enough to be in your show now?" he asked. Well, of course, he was, and with D.A.'s help, I learned how to do the Ray Floyd walk. He has a distinctive hip swivel and takes short steps and leans forward slightly, almost as though he were bucking a head wind. He also has a habit of constantly touching the bill of his visor with his right hand. Raymond's swing is unique. He takes it back to the inside, gets the club slightly laid off, then quickly gets back to a great position at the ball. After impact, he glares at that ball as if to say, Don't you dare miss the fairway or the green or I'm taking you out of play.

I don't imitate Raymond chipping, because I'd have to knock the ball in the hole every time, then point my finger at the cup and fire a bullet at it. Fact is, I'm non-violent. I also can't chip that well.

I suppose if I'm going to continue to do impressions, I'll have to incorporate the current stars in my routine. The audience only responds if they know the swing and have seen it repeated a thousand times. Nowadays, if I did one

of my old reliables, Doug Sanders, it would be like doing
Colonel Sanders because Doug's not as visible as he was in
his prime. With no recognition, there's no laughter. So I'll
probably work on a Corey Pavin and a John Daly and a
Paul Azinger. But it won't be quite the same.

The truth is, I started doing impersonations because I
idolized all the guys that I was mimicking. And as much as
I respect all the top current players, I don't have the same
feeling for them as I do the older players. It's just not
healthy to idolize guys you're trying to beat every week.

CHAPTER 6

Major Memories

SPEAKING OF TRYING to beat guys—I hope to rectify one glaring disappointment in my professional career before I'm done playing: I want to win a major championship. You just can't overemphasize the importance of a major to a golfer's career.

No matter what a player does the rest of his playing days, he will be most remembered for winning major titles. The best recent example is Tom Kite. He was the all-time leading money-winner on Tour, with sixteen titles, a marvelous record in the Ryder Cup matches, and probably the best record of consistently excellent play in the last two decades, yet when his record was discussed he always had to hear, "Yeah, but . . ."

That all changed when he won the U.S. Open at Pebble Beach in 1992. Any implied asterisks after Kite's name were erased with that victory.

The importance of a major championship is even more pronounced if a popular player wins just one. Think of broadcasters such as Dave Marr and Ken Venturi. Every time those guys are introduced, it's as if their names contained five or six words instead of just two. It's never simply Dave Marr. It's always former-PGA-champion Dave Marr, or former-U.S. Open-champion Ken Venturi. Instantly, a hyphenated adjective appears in front of their name, giving them a credibility unquestioned by the golfing public.

I've never won any of the top four tournaments, but I have had opportunities, and I'd like to share with you the feeling of seeing your name at the top of a major championship leaderboard, and the mental challenge of dealing with that pressure.

In hindsight, perhaps my best-ever chance to win a major was at the 1983 PGA at Riviera Country Club in Los Angeles. Broadcasters always talk about going out early Sunday, posting a low number, and letting the boys shoot at it. Johnny Miller came from nowhere to win with a final-round 63 in the 1973 U.S. Open at Oakmont, and Gary Player's final-round 64 at Augusta in 1978 snatched the Masters from a trio of players. That's what I had a chance to do at Riviera—fire early and hope the rest would fall back.

I began the last round of the PGA eight shots behind third-round leader Hal Sutton, and by the time I teed off on the last hole, I was in need of just one more birdie to have an excellent chance of winning the tournament. But let me back up to explain how I got there.

Going into that week, I was hitting the ball terribly and really struggling with my swing. My friend Jim Hardy, an excellent instructor who played the Tour in the 1970s, was watching me on the driving range after the final practice round on Wednesday, and he said, "Peter, you have the club shut at the top and you are laid off. I want you to try to get the club more square, so next week when you're at home, try cupping your left wrist at the top of your back-swing."

I made an exaggerated swing and said, "Like this?"

"That's perfect," he said.

Well, as with all major swing changes, it felt horrible, and when I tried the new swing I pushed the shot about 100 yards to the right.

Jim laughed and said, "Believe it or not, that looks better."

I continued with it and hit about ten more foul balls into the right-field bleachers, places even the peanut-vendor wouldn't go near, and Jim said, "Okay, put that thought away and work on it next week when you get home."

I said, "Don't worry. I can get this by tomorrow." Now, maybe that's one of the things that sets Tour players apart from other golfers. I don't want to sound cocky here, but we sometimes feel we're invincible. I thought, hey, I need to make a change, so I'll do it right now and I'll be fine by tomorrow. I took a totally positive attitude. Rather than worrying about how high the rough was that week, or that if I hit any crooked balls off the fairway I'd just have to wedge it out, I felt that I could incorporate the change overnight and then hit the ball well all week. Hardy proba-bly went to dinner that night regretting ever opening his mouth, but I had made a decision: I would go with the new swing.

The first two rounds, I hit it pretty well and shot 73–68, but I was ten back of Sutton, who opened with a PGA record 65–66. I started the third round by knocking my tee shot out of bounds on the first hole, which is easy to do at Riviera, but still shot a respectable 70. After 54 holes, I was in about twentieth place, just hoping to move up in the last round and get the benefits that come with a high finish in a major, such as an exemption into the Masters, the Open, and the PGA.

In Sunday's final round, I birdied the second, fourth, and eighth holes, and thought, hey, this is getting interesting. But I especially remember the ninth. Jack Lemmon was walking with me; when Jack's there he keeps a very low profile, but I always know he's there. It comforts me to know my partner is watching and making sure I do everything right. On the ninth, I had driven into the right rough, but it was the best angle of approach because that green angles from short right to long left, and I had a straight shot at the pin. I hit an eight-iron, and although there were a couple hundred people around, Lemmon was right behind me and he has that distinctive voice. The only thing I heard when the ball was in the air was Jack saying, "Yes."

The shot, as we say, was hit so straight at the flag that I had to lean sideways to follow the flight of the ball, and I remember perfectly hearing Lemmon, with his cigarillo hanging from his lower lip, going "Yes."

I made the putt to complete a front nine of 31, then ran off three more birdies in a row on 10, 11, and 12 to go seven under for the day. When you start bunching birdies in the last round of a major championship, you leave skid marks all over the fairways from passing people so quickly. At that point I was definitely in the chase, although Jack Nicklaus was also putting on one of his patented last-round charges.

The spell finally broke when I bogied number 13, but I birdied the par-five 17th to return to seven under par for the day and nine under for the tournament. Sutton, I believe, was at minus ten, with about five holes to play. A birdie at the last hole would tie me for the lead, or even give me a chance to win if Hal stumbled coming home.

As I walked to the 18th tee, however, I let myself down and failed to think like a champion. Rather than roll up my sleeves and tell myself I *was* going to birdie the hole to win, I thought about what I *didn't* want to do. I didn't want to make a bogey. As a result, I made a very scared swing with the driver, and blocked it slightly into the right rough. That's Deadsville on 18 at Riviera, because huge eucalyptus trees block the entrance to the green. I had to wedge back to the fairway, then hit another wedge, which rolled to the back of the green. I two-putted for a bogey.

I had shot a 65 in the last round of a major championship, and ended up at third alone, two behind Sutton and one behind Nicklaus, who closed with a 66. It was my best showing ever in one of golf's four biggest events.

So did I feel great? Hardly. I was as disappointed as I'd ever been, because I hadn't *thought* like a champion at a critical moment. I had tried to protect my position instead of throwing caution to the wind and going after the victory like I deserved it. It's just so hard to get into position to win a major title, that when you're right there and you fail, it's a horrible letdown.

Three years later, I had another chance to win the PGA, but what happened to me that week is long forgotten behind the dramatics that took place between my playing partners in the final threesome.

The 1986 PGA at Inverness Country Club in Toledo, Ohio, will probably be seen through the rear-view mirror of history as the beginning of the Greg Norman Curse. But

at the time, it looked like the blooming of the Greg Norman Era.

That was the year that Norman "won" what was called
the 54-hole Slam, which meant that he led all four majors
after 54 holes. He had led the Masters and U.S. Open, only
to be overtaken by two great players, at Augusta by Jack
Nicklaus, and at the Open by Raymond Floyd. Coincidentally, both players were the oldest to win those championships at the time of their victories.

If Greg had self-doubts because of the lost leads, they
seemed to disappear with his victory in the British Open at
Turnberry, in which a marvelous final round stretched a
three-round one-stroke margin into a five-shot triumph.

So when Norman finished three rounds of the 1986
PGA in eight under par for a commanding lead, most
armchair observers were predicting his second major victory in as many months. I certainly wouldn't have bet
against Greg as I teed off with him and Bob Tway in the
final threesome on Sunday. Tway was in second place, four
shots back, and I was six back at two-under-par 208.

I don't recall the exact scores, but none of us burned up
the front nine and Norman still had at least a four-shot lead
after 63 holes. He was hitting the ball so well, though, that
I expected him to go on a birdie tear any minute. I remember telling my caddie Mike that the only one who could
beat Greg Norman was Greg Norman. If one thing was
bugging Greg that week, it was how much backspin he was
putting on the ball. He would land his iron shots by the
hole, and they would just zip back off the front of the
greens.

He was using a new balata ball noted for exceptional
spin, I remember, and with the hard, fast greens at Inverness, the only way he could keep his iron shots close was

to fly them to the backs of the greens, which is a dangerous proposition.

On the 10th hole, a short par-four that is played with a one-iron and a wedge, Greg's wedge shot landed about six inches from the cup and sucked back to the front of the green and into the second cut of fringe. He failed to get it up and down and made bogey. The backspin in that case cost him two shots, from a birdie to a bogey.

Then on the 11th, he drove the ball into a divot, couldn't get to the ball cleanly, and left his second shot in a bunker. He could do no better than a double-bogey. He'd lost three shots of a four-shot lead, and Tway and I were back in the tournament. We were both just one or two shots behind at that point. Although I felt positive about my own game, I still thought Greg had his game under control because he was striking the ball so well. He was driving it long and straight, his irons were right at the flag, and he was putting well. The bad holes at 10 and 11 had not affected his demeanor at all.

Greg and I talked a lot during that round, because we're good friends, and I saw nothing in his behavior that indicated he wasn't going to win the golf tournament.

As it happened, though, Tway made a birdie late in the back nine, and by the time we reached the 18th hole, he had pulled even with Norman. I had made a string of pars and was still three shots back. I knew it would take a miracle for me to catch them, and while a miracle did indeed occur at the 72nd hole, it was reserved for another member of our threesome.

The last hole at Inverness is a short par-four, maybe 330 yards, and all of us hit irons off the tee. Greg and I were perfect in the middle of the fairway, and Bob was in the right rough, which was dead on that hole, because the pin was cut on the front and there was no way for him to get to it. He had no chance to keep the ball on the green, so he did the next best thing, which was to put it in the front bunker.

I sensed nothing but confidence from Get as he hit his second shot. He hit a wedge perfectly, about six feet from the hole, but once again the rotation got him. The ball zipped back into the front fringe, just as it had done on the 10th hole.

Now, although I can't put spin on the ball like Greg, I didn't want to do the same thing, so I took a nine-iron and hit the shot with more of a half-speed swing, which automatically takes some of the rotation off the ball. I tried not to pinch it, but just to make nice contact. The ball landed twelve feet from the pin, and stopped on a dime.

I needed to make my putt, and Norman and Tway had to make sixes, for me to get in a playoff, and while I never wish bad luck on another golfer—I believe it pisses off the gods of golf—I'll admit I was concocting a scenario for exactly that as I walked up to the green. Anyone would do the same. Tway's bunker shot was to a downhill pin, and if he got too aggressive he could either leave it in the bunker, or blast it long and three-putt the slick green.

Norman was far less likely to make a six, but you never know how the ball is going to come out of that long grass, and a poor chip could lead to a three-putt. Then if I rolled in the birdie, we would all be tied at 279. As far-fetched as that sequence of events seems, it's the kind of thought process that goes through every player's mind when he or she still has a remote chance to win.

When I got to the green, I marked my ball, and noticed that Greg had a very poor lie, and Bob had a difficult bunker shot, although his lie was all right. I still thought, Maybe, just maybe.

Tway didn't take long to hit his bunker shot, and when it first came out I thought it was a good one that would roll probably ten feet past. Then it looked good enough to make no worse than five, which meant my chances were done. And then his ball hit the pin and disappeared.

I looked at Bob, who was in total shock for an instant, then he started jumping up and down in the bunker, pumping his fists in the air. Then I looked at Greg, and to his credit, his expression didn't change a bit. He maintained the same straight face he'd had walking to the green, and went about the business of studying his chip shot.

Remember, in 1986, Greg Norman had no sense of being cursed. Tway's miracle preceded those of Larry Mize at Augusta and Robert Gamez at Bay Hill and David Frost at New Orleans, and even the great playoff comeback of Mark Calcavecchia at the British Open.

Although many fans watching at home surely realized what Tway's shot meant, that he had holed a shot from off the green on the last hole to win a major championship (a feat that happens about once every quarter of a century, or at least until Larry Mize did it at Augusta eight months later), what it meant to me was that my chance of winning the PGA was over.

I never once thought that Greg wasn't going to win that tournament until Tway's shot went in the hole. And if it hadn't gone in, and Greg had won at Inverness, I honestly believe that he would have totally dominated golf for about the next five years. That bunker shot set off a chain of unbelievable events, almost as though they were conjured up in a black pot of magical spells and thrown on Greg as a curse. Certainly no player in the history of golf has had to bite his lip harder than Greg Norman at the odd twists of fate.

Because I'm a friend of Greg's, I've been asked several

times what those setbacks have done to him as a person. I feel qualified to answer the question because I've been with him after all five of those tournaments—the four-holed shots and the playoff loss at the British Open—and not once did I see him treat anybody with disrespect or unkindness, but, rather, with the compassion of a true gentleman. But I do believe those losses have made Greg question his own game, and his immense talent, and that is a shame.

Greg Norman is good for golf, because he plays with such bravado. He's confident and flamboyant, and he hits shots that other players can't hit. He's also a little like the great Walter Hagen, in that he can lead the golf tournament, throw the party that night and entertain everybody till the wee hours, then wake up the next day and beat your brains out.

Who knows how long his great run in the late 1980s would have gone had he not suffered those gut-wrenching losses?

But because he is a tough competitor, I believe we'll see Greg Norman win many more championships, and more majors as well, before he takes off his spikes for the last time.

One recent major championship memory has absolutely nothing to do with my performance in the tournament, but in an unlikely way it does speak to the popularity of golf.

Several friends meet us at the Masters each year, people from different parts of the country that I've befriended from various pro-ams, and I jokingly call them the Masters Mafia. We have an annual barbecue with them on the Tuesday before the tournament, and dinner on Sunday afterwards. Among this group are Peter and Jean Humphrey, and Dick Bruno from New London, Connecticut. Now, Dick is a bachelor and a fun-loving guy, who is not averse to doing a little "mingling" when he's in Augusta.

On the Wednesday night before the opening round last year, Dick found himself at a popular watering hole called T-Bones, where he managed to introduce himself to two attractive women. They accepted his invitation to buy them dinner. Feeling no pain, Dick was throwing more pitches than Roger Clemens, hoping, of course, that his witty repartee would lure one or both of them into romance, at least for the night. He told them he was a friend of mine and that he would be at the tournament all week. He then gave them the name of his hotel and the room number, just in case they were curious.

Well, they apparently had other plans, because they thanked him for the dinner and excused themselves. Dick was satisfied he'd given it his best shot, so he cabbed it back to his hotel and crashed. About midnight, as he was in a deep sleep dreaming of what might have been, Dick was awakened by a knock on his door. He stumbled out of bed and opened it to find his two lovely dinner companions smiling brightly and asking if they could come in. Dick said they looked even better in the shadowy light of his room than they had in the brightly lit restaurant, but then don't we all?

One of them sat on the bed with him and started to express her gratitude for the wonderful dinner, and the other coyly stood over by the dresser, leafing through the Spectravision guide. She said she was looking for a good adult movie they might watch. Dick was thinking, Holy Moly, how good does it get? I'm here at the Masters with two gorgeous women who are absolutely crazy about me.

About then, the woman who was standing said to Dick, "Look, I'm parked in a handicapped zone and if we're going to stay a while I better move my car." She quickly left the room. The woman on the bed with Dick continued her friendly ways, then suddenly sat up and said, "I left my purse in the car. Let me go get it and I'll be right back."

When she left, Dick quickly brushed his teeth and flossed and gargled and performed other hygienically-proper procedures, then returned to bed awaiting the fulfillment of all his fantasies.

After a few minutes, he started to get nervous. He couldn't understand what was taking them so long. Then he realized he had over a thousand dollars in his wallet, which was on the dresser. He jumped up and checked it. The money was all there, as were all his credit cards.

Then he thought of his car—but, no, the keys were right where he'd left them.

Another ten minutes passed. Finally, the light flashed on. His Masters tournament badge—probably the most cherished ticket in all of sports—had been placed on a side table. It was gone!

Poor Dick was down and out in Augusta: trick-rolled for his Masters badge, with no way to replace it.

But Dick's luck wasn't all bad that night. When he realized his dilemma, he went next door and awakened Eddy Ellis, a business associate of mine who had come down from Portland. As Eddy listened to Dick's tale of woe, he nonchalantly said, "Don't worry about it, Dick. I just happened to stumble onto an extra ticket today. You can have it."

Postscript: Dick gave me permission to tell this story in the hope that other die-hard male golf fans will use better judgment. He sums it up this way. "In Augusta, in April, the Masters is all anyone cares about. Money, cars, and sex aren't even a close second."

CHAPTER 7

The Human Hinge

I'VE MENTIONED JACK LEMMON enough times by now that I suppose I ought to introduce him properly.

My first personal contact with Jack was a phone call. I was home in Portland and I happened to be on the throne, reading the sports page, which is one of my favorite things to do. Anyway, the phone rang and Jan answered it and this voice said, "I understand Peter Jacobsen needs a golf lesson and I'm going to give it to him."

Jan said, "Who *is* this?" because her first thought was that it was a crank call.

The voice said, "It's the Human Hinge."

I yelled from the toilet, "Who is it?"

Jan said, "Honey, it's for you. He says it's the Human Hinge."

"Who the hell's that?" I grumbled, and went back to studying batting averages for the Portland Beavers.

Jan asked, "Could I have a name, please?"

The voice said, "It's Jack Lemmon."

So Jan covered the phone and said, in an urgent tone, "It's Jack Lemmon!"

Well, I didn't even sit up. I just kind of slid off the pot and did the turkey-trot over to the phone—the sort of thing you can do in your own home, even if the kids do look at you funny—and sure enough it was Jack Lemmon. I knew the voice immediately. And he said, "I understand you need a partner in the Crosby, someone who can carry you around, and I'm looking for one. Let's play together."

It turns out my accountant, George Mack, had been paired with Lemmon in a pro-am and told him I was a young player on the Tour and that I liked to have fun in pro-ams. Lemmon's the same way. As hard as Jack tries to win, he never forgets that the real purpose is to have fun, and that's what we've done, ever since 1983. It's been a great marriage in every respect. I know that Lemmon's missed the pro-am cut in that tournament every year since the Emancipation Proclamation—which includes the ten years he's been my partner—but we've had such a blast together it doesn't really matter.

Mark my words, however. Not only do I believe we will make the cut one year, I believe we'll win the doggone thing. I really do. In fact, I advise all readers of this book to rush to Las Vegas and see if you can get a future bet on us at about ten million to one.

Just how bad does Lemmon want to make the cut at Pebble? Well, Jack has said he'd trade both his Oscars if that happened, but I think he's lying. He'd only give up one.

I have so many stories about Lemmon at the Crosby (now called the AT&T Pebble Beach National Pro-Am), that it's hard to choose only a few.

One that stands out, because it was on national TV, was the Infamous Hanging Ice Plant Wedge Shot at the 16th hole at Cypress Point, the most notorious golf hole in the world. But I have to offer some preliminaries to that moment, because the whole day was a riot.

Jack and I were paired with Greg Norman and Clint Eastwood, so naturally we had a huge gallery and there were a lot of cameras clicking away at Clint and Jack. Every now and then, Greg and I would jump into the picture just so we wouldn't develop an inferiority complex. Anyway, we were on the 11th tee at Cypress, which is a congestion point, and play was backed up by a couple of groups. The foursome right in front of us included Jack Nicklaus, Dee Keaton, Hale Irwin, and President Ford—with Secret Service agents in tow—and, of course, there were paramedics and ambulances nearby in case the former Commander-in-Chief shanked any one-irons and flattened a few galleryites (just kidding, Mr. President).

Now, what many people don't know is that Greg Norman is a real prankster. He's very serious about his golf game, but he loves to have fun and play practical jokes.

So we were in this bottleneck, with about a fifteen-minute wait, and Lemmon snuck off in the direction of the Port-a-Potty. Greg and Clint and I all looked at one another, and I made a throwing motion. My companions enthusiastically nodded. We crept up to the crapper, which was constructed from hard plastic, and we all went into our best Nolan Ryan windups and threw our golf balls at the can as hard as we could.

Bang! Bang! Bang! It sounded like three pistol shots. I half-expected the Secret Service agents to draw their sidearms. But instead there was dead silence, and the next thing we saw was a sweet little lady, who'd peeked her head out the door and asked, "Is it safe to come out now?" She looked like she'd seen a ghost.

Then Lemmon walked around from behind the can, where he'd been standing talking to a friend, and said,

"What the hell are you guys doing?" The three of us just stood there, like cats with cream on our whiskers. We were all embarrassed, but there wasn't much to say. So Jack went over to the lady, put his arm around her, and apologized for his choice in golfing partners, while the Three Stooges shuffled back to the tee, stifling hysteria. It wasn't as if we could pretend it was an accident. At least a thousand people standing nearby had seen us do it, and most of them hadn't known we thought Lemmon was the one inside. Oh, well.

That poor lady probably needed professional counseling before she was able to use outdoor plumbing again.

By the time we reached the 16th, there had been some serious male-bonding going on. As usual, there was another big backup on the tee, which affords a player plenty of time to appreciate the beauty of the hole, and just how big the Pacific Ocean really is. As a golfer standing on that tee, you see a couple of measly acres of grass and a million miles of water. As Bill Murray said during play last year, "And that's just the *top* of it."

The wind always howls, usually dead in your face, and rumor has it the seals down on the rocks below raise one flipper to call for a fair catch on all the balls dropping over the cliff. In other words, it's scary as hell.

The carry to the green is 215 yards, and depending on the direction of the wind, the pros will normally use a driver, three-wood, or one-iron to reach it. Because on most days Jack can't carry it to the green, he normally plays to an inlet of grass to the left, and then hits a wedge for his second shot. On this day the wind was so strong in our faces that none of us went for the green. Norman and Eastwood and I laid up successfully to the left.

Then it was time for the Human Hinge to show his stuff. Jack took a long pull on his cigarillo, blew the smoke into the air to test the wind, then made a horrible pass at the

ball. I've seen better swings on a condemned playground.
He hit a fluttering quail which barely trickled off the grass
and got hung up in the ice plant on the edge of the cliff.
It was a mere sixty-foot dropoff to the rocks and crashing
surf below.

I assumed Jack would just shake his pom-poms and
cheer us on for the rest of the hole, but Eastwood, who
sprinkles testosterone on his Wheaties every morning, said
"C'mon, Jack, you can't just leave the son of a bitch sittin'
there flippin' you off. You've got to play that mother."

Keep in mind there were two groups on the tee watching us, another three or four thousand in the gallery, and
about twenty million more on television. Obviously, there
was some male ego on the line here. So Lemmon swallowed hard and grabbed his infamous L-Wedge, designed
for lob shots. When he started to crawl over the edge, I got
nervous. Let me emphasize: this was a dangerous situation.
We're talking ice plant growing out of the edge of a rock
wall with certain death below. And here went one of the
world's greatest actors to hit it.

With trepidation in my voice, I said, "Partner, Hollywood and the movie-going public need you for your next
film far more than I need you to make a nine on this hole."

But Eastwood didn't want to hear it. He said, "C'mon,
Jack, I'll help you."

At this point, Lemmon didn't need coercing. With a
gleam in his eye and a mischievous smile, he started his
climb down the cliff. Clint instinctively grabbed Jack by
the belt and back of his pants. I grabbed Eastwood's arm,
Norman grabbed mine, and his caddy Pete Bender grabbed
his. Instantly, we had formed a human chain of safety. Talk
about safe sex, well, this was safe golf. I don't think any of
us was wearing a rubber at the time, but it might not have
been a bad idea.

Although what we were doing broke about six rules of golf, that wasn't our primary concern at the time. After a few tense moments, Lemmon chopped at the ball and it miraculously popped out in the fairway. We all crawled back up to safer terrain, laughing our butts off, while the crowd gave Jack a huge ovation. I remember Lemmon pumping his fist in the air, and the rest of us giving him high-fives like he'd just won an Olympic gold medal.

Jack now had about 70 yards to the hole, and his adrenal glands were pumping wide open as the world pulled for him to complete this miraculous recovery. He took a couple of waggles, drew the wedge back slowly . . . and shanked it into the ocean.

Which is where the damn ball belonged in the first place, if you really think about it.

There's another story about Lemmon and an outhouse that I have to tell, although Jack will want to kill me for including it. He'll say something like, "Gee, Peter, thanks for all the mentions in your book. It's just unfortunate that every story you told about me took place on or near the growler."

This one occurred during a pro-am at the Fred Meyer Challenge. Jack was playing with me and he hit his drive in the trees on the 11th hole at Portland Golf Club. As he went in there to hit it, he told me he had to make a pit stop. So he cracked a five-wood out of the trees, it hit a tree limb and bounced back out into the fairway, and all the people applauded. Lemmon then handed the club to his caddy and politely got in line behind about eight people at the Port-a-John.

A television camera had been focused on the play, and the funny thing was that all the people lined up there had just applauded this recovery shot by an Academy Award winner, yet nobody would give him cuts in the line so he could do his business and rejoin his foursome.

Finally, my wife's Aunt Eileen, who recognized the situation, said, "Jack, you can cut in here and get back to your group." Jack thanked her for being so thoughtful and went in and started to drop trow. Just then, Aunt Eileen pulled the door open and said, "Oh, Jack. Can I get a picture?"

So Jack, holding his pants up, stuck his head out like a dog peering out the side window of a station wagon, and gave her a polite, albeit beleaguered smile. One of the broadcasters, who didn't realize his mike was open, said on the air, "I think she just snapped a picture of his Willy."

I'll bet I've watched the tape of that twenty times, and it cracks me up every time.

Jack Lemmon takes a lot of ridicule as a golfer, and he is as gracious about it as he is with all the honors that have come his way. It's not easy to smile when you get publicly humiliated each year in a golf tournament that means as much to you as the AT&T does to Jack. Lemmon has said many times that he would feel less anxiety opening on Broadway in *Hamlet* with no rehearsals than he feels hitting that first tee shot at Pebble Beach.

Every year, it seems, the television cameras catch him in horrible predicaments. They must use the same crew to shoot *Emergency* and *Rescue 911*. I'm convinced CBS's cameramen wait to find Lemmon in trouble before they put him on the air. It's sort of sadistic, but it's probably good for ratings.

Jack's wife Felicia once put together a "low-light" reel of all the bad shots he'd hit in the AT&T, and it ran longer than *Dances with Wolves*. Several years ago, Byron Nelson analyzed Jack's swing for the television audience and found eight things wrong with it. They ran the tape backwards and forwards, over and over. Bing Crosby was in the booth with Byron and he said, "My God, he looks like he's basting a chicken." And Phil Harris said, "This guy's been in more bunkers than Eva Braun."

One time, it took Jack eleven strokes to reach the 18th green at Pebble Beach. He'd had intimate contact with all the elements—water, sand, earth, wind, and fire—by the time he got there, but he refused to pick up. He eventually ended up with a thirty-foot putt for a 12, so, of course, he plumb-bobbed it. He then looked back over his shoulder at his caddy, and said, "Which way does it break?"

And the caddy said, "Who cares?"

But nobody ever laughs *at* Jack, they always laugh *with* him, because he's such a warm, wonderful person. And if I don't ease up on him, he'll dump me next year and team up with Freddie Couples.

CHAPTER 8

The Man on the Bag

ONE OF THE RUNNING JOKES on the Tour is to refer to the player/caddy relationship as a "marriage." When Bruce Edwards quit working for Greg Norman in 1992 and went back to Tom Watson, they kidded them about getting divorced.

This analogy is stretching it a bit. While having a compatible caddy is important to any player, it doesn't hold a candle to having a good marriage. And if each time a player and caddy split up was actually a divorce, most Tour players would have been "married" more times than Zsa Zsa and Liz combined.

I've been extremely fortunate in both respects. I've had the same great wife since 1976, and the same great caddy since 1978. My caddy, Mike Cowan, certainly knows that my wife is vastly more important to me than he is, and a whole lot better-looking. That said, however, I also feel I've got the best caddy in the business: he's extremely professional, he's never been late for work one day in the last fifteen years, he's a good player himself who understands the physical and mental aspects of the game, and he knows exactly how to handle me.

I met Mike at Silverado Country Club in Napa, California, in the fall of 1977. This guy who looked like a cross between Grizzly Adams and Jerry Garcia introduced himself to me and said he was impressed with my game. I saw Mike a few other times, but he didn't start packing for me until the Heritage Classic the next spring. He was sort of rolling the dice with me because I was an unproven second-year player at the time, and had won only twelve grand as a rookie. But Mike saw potential in me, and he had qualities I liked. The main one was that he was very quiet. One way I release nervous energy on the course is to be a motor-mouth, and the last thing I needed was Gabby Hayes on the bag.

I had a brief taste of caddying myself when I was in college, so I understood firsthand the aspects of the job. Jan's brother, Mike Davis, had played the Tour in 1974 and 1975, and I'd caddied for him in a few West Coast tournaments. It had given me a valuable first peek into the world of professional golf.

A better comparison of the caddy/player relationship would be that of an executive assistant to a businessman. The employer wants things done a certain way, and it's his assistant's job to see that those idiosyncrasies are catered to, without having to ask a lot of questions.

Every golfer has his own quirks, and it's the caddy's job to adapt to them. Some players want a total yardage to the pin read to them, such as 176 yards. Others want it broken down, such as 138 to the front, 15 to the swale, and another 23 to the pin. Players frequently want a yardage behind the hole, also, so they'll know how much room they have before the ball goes bounding off into the great unknown.

The famous streaker incident at the 1985 British Open. Poor Sandy Lyle had to take second billing—he only won the tournament.

Undress of a different sort: Curtis Strange and I sell off his jeans at the 1989 Fred Meyer Challenge charity auction. Greg Norman seems to be considering a bid himself. (*Photo by Kristin Finnegan*)

The Infamous Hanging Ice Plant Wedge Shot at Pebble Beach. From right to left, Jack Lemmon, Clint Eastwood, me, Greg Norman, and Greg's caddy Pete Bender.
(*Photo by Dave Button*)

The Human Hinge: Jack Lemmon
(*Photo by Tom Treick*)

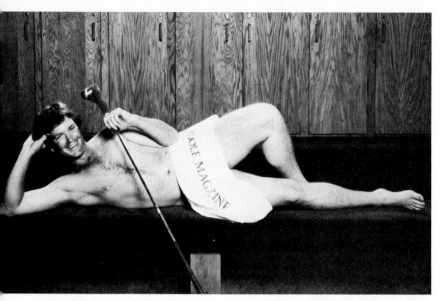

Weird bulges and strange tan lines: my *Golf* magazine center-fold. Keith Fergus, Greg Norman, Payne Stewart and Rex Caldwell also got photographed—but I was the lucky one with staples in my navel. (*Photograph © 1983 by Jules Alexander*)

My best times as a golfer have been partnering with Arnold Palmer. (*Photo by Mike Lloyd*)

Peter's impressions: Counter-clockwise from above, as Johnny Miller; as Tom Kite; preparing myself for Craig Stadler; Stadler in full swing. (*Photos by Tom Treick*)

There's always fun at The Fred Meyer Challenge. Left to right, Mark Calcavecchia, Curtis Strange, Andy Bean, me, Bob Tway and Arnold Palmer. (*Photo by Tom Treick*)

From left to right, Mark Lye, Payne Stewart and me—the one, the only, Jake Trout and the Flounders. Huey Lewis, eat your heart out. (*Photo by Kristin Finnegan*)

Michael Jordan's reaction to my comment that I will be playing in the NBA someday. (*Photo by Chick Natella*)

Bill Murray and me getting psychologically prepared for the Western Open Celebrity Shoot-Out. Somehow it worked. (*Courtesy of Peter de Young and the Western Open*)

With Bob Hope after winning the 1990 Bob Hope Chrysler
Classic. (*Photograph copyright © 1990 by Mitchell Haddad*)

Mike Cowan, the best caddy in the business.
(*Photograph copyright © 1990 by Mitchell Haddad*)

With my dad, Erling.

The Jacobsens. Left to right: Kristen, Jan, Amy, Mickey and me.

The one absolute imperative for caddies is to be able to add properly. Those who played hooky in the second grade had better pack a pocket-calculator. One bad shot can ruin a tournament or even turn an entire year around, so giving an incorrect yardage is a capital offense for a caddy. It's also important for him to be a clock-watcher, and to keep his player constantly updated on the time, to make sure the golfer's pre-round regimen of practice and other matters can be completed comfortably before the starting time.

In my rookie year, at the Southern Open in Columbus, Georgia, I was on the driving range warming up before the first round. I had told my caddy to keep an eye on the first tee—which is over a hill and out of sight of the range—so he could inform me when the group ahead of us had teed off. Well, he wasn't paying close attention and when I walked up to the tee, my playing partners had already hit and were walking down the fairway. I was slapped with a two-stroke penalty, and ended up missing the cut by one. My caddy was slapped with his walking papers.

As I said, Mike works well for me primarily because of his personality. I don't want a cheerleader out there. I want a reliable guy who understands how I want to manage my time, has a good feel for the mental side of the game, and will put up with my stream-of-consciousness ramblings as we're walking along. The fact that Mike knows my golf swing, and can help spot flaws if I ask him to, is stricly a bonus.

Mike and I have a calm, professional relationship, but there are those, such as Lee Trevino and his long-time caddy Herman Mitchell, who succeed as partners despite an occasional eruption. They lob a lot of barbs back and forth, which are fun to hear, but this only gets Lee revved up, which makes him play better. I've seen Lee hit a couple bad shots and say, "Herman, you can't add." And Herman will say, "Well, you can't play golf."

Lee likes to tell his amateur partners to play their putts to break toward the side of the hole where Herman is standing, because he's so big the green will slope toward him. The bottom line is that Lee wins everything in sight, and Herman's so famous he has his own endorsements. Theirs is an unconventional but highly successful business partnership.

The best Tour caddies, like the best players, work their tails off. Contrary to the perception that the Tour player's life is a fairly cushy berth, there're thousands of hours of hard work behind every victory. The public sees the pro with the winner's check and the crystal trophy and the devoted wife smiling up at him and thinks, "Tough life." But they don't see the long hours of preparation and, in some cases, years of frustration and disappointment, that led up to that moment.

When Mike and I are on the road, it's a seven-day work week, with us usually arriving at the course about eight or nine A.M. and leaving at six or seven in the evening. A lot of times there's a Monday outing, followed by a Tuesday practice round and a Merrill Lynch Shoot-Out, and another pro-am on Wednesday. All of these functions are preceded by a bucket of balls and a session of chipping and putting, and then the same after the round. Squeezed in between are news interviews and autographs to sign and people to talk to.

Mike is always with me when I'm practicing, and he's on standby when I'm doing the other stuff, because as soon as it's over we'll practice some more.

Thursday through Sunday, there's less of the outside activities, but that's when the mental stress of competition begins. I don't hit a lot of practice balls during the tournament, unless I'm struggling with my swing or feel a certain part of my game needs work, but I will spend a lot of time fine-tuning my short game. Mike can be helpful there by watching me practice, and keeping his eye on certain keys I work on from week to week. He also helps keep me focused, because I have been known to get caught up in high jinks with other players.

Once at Westchester, Mike and I had a flare-up over something that was my fault, but the story tells you a little about both of us.

The driving range was being used for parking, so we were using a fairway on the other course to practice. I had my own practice balls, which Mike was shagging for me. He had the flu, but he hadn't said anything about it. Anyway, a bunch of us had hit a lot of balls and our session had kind of deteriorated to where everybody was hitting trick shots. I started doing my swing impersonations, and we were all laughing. Those kinds of relaxed times when you can enjoy your friendships with the other players don't happen enough, and I remember having a great time. I was hitting Johnny Miller six-irons and Miller Barber wedge shots, and we were all yukking it up.

Suddenly, Mike walked in from the landing area and got right up in my face and said, "Look, are you gonna practice or are you gonna screw around, because if you're not gonna work, I've got better things to do!" Then he turned around and stomped back out. I could tell he wasn't feeling well because his breath melted my visor.

Needless to say, I got back to serious practicing, and although I got on him later about how he had handled the situation, he was right. If I was going to screw around, it should have been on my own time. But that's another reason why Mike is good for me. Whereas I have a tendency to get carried away with having fun or telling jokes, Mike never lets me forget why we're there—and that is to play good golf and to win tournaments.

As I said, Mike's a good player in his own right, a solid five-handicap. He has such a simple, effective swing that he can drop the bag after caddying three or four hours, take one practice swing, and flush a three-iron right at the flag. That's not easy under any circumstances, much less wearing a jumpsuit or a caddy bib!

He also has a little competitive fire. We like to do something that's strictly against Tour regulations, but is always entertaining. In practice rounds, Mike often challenges one of the pros in our group to a one-hole match for a few bucks. We usually choose a par-three, where he can hit one quick shot off the tee, putt a couple times, and then pretend that it never happened, so I won't get fined. (As a two-time member of the Tour Policy Board, I'll probably get fined just for telling the story here.)

Mike absolutely owns Curtis Strange in these one-hole bets. I don't think he's ever lost to Curtis. And overall, against guys like D. A. Weibring and Dave Eichelberger and Tom Byrum, I'd say he's won about 75 percent of the time.

A couple of times, we've had fun with our pro-am team. In 1991 at Bay Hill, a daughter of one of my amateurs was caddying for her dad, and she was a college golfer. I really wanted to see her hit the ball, so on the 18th hole, knowing her dad and the other amateurs wouldn't mind, I asked her to play Mike in a one-hole match. I winked at Mike and said, "Five dollars says she beats you."

She used her dad's clubs, and I caddied for her. Mike, of course, had to caddy for himself. Now, in 1990, the last

hole at Bay Hill was rated as the most difficult hole on the
Tour, but she got right up by the green in two and made
a bogey. Meanwhile, my faithful caddy, after packing all
day, took out my driver, ripped it long down the right side,
then froze a three-iron in there about twelve feet. The
crowd went nuts and I lost five bucks.

My amateurs always like Mike, anyway, because he's
willing to give them yardages and read putts for them.
Mike appreciates, as I do, that pro-am day in the various
cities is the biggest day of the year for local amateur golfers.
It's their one chance to play with the big boys. However,
it never fails that some high-handicapper in the group, a
guy who has no idea how far he hits the various clubs
anyway, will start really getting into the yardage thing.
Mike will be walking off a yardage for me on a par-five, for
instance, pacing forward from a 297 sprinkler, and the
amateur will be back just ahead of the ladies' tee somewhere, and say, "How much have I got, Mike?"

Mike will patiently pace back to the guy's ball and say,
"Well, you've got three-forty-one to the front and another
twelve to the pin. Three-fifty-three, Mr. Oglethorp."

And Mr. Oglethorp will say, "So what do you think?"

Of course, Mike is thinking, You can't get there by
bus, pal, but he'll say, patiently, "I think it's a three-
wood."

The real art of it is to give the guy the yardage without
ever cracking a smile. Three-forty-one to the front, and
another twelve to the pin. I love that.

The guys who caddy for consistent money-winners—players who are always in the solid six-figures in annual prize
money—can make a good living. Five or six of them have
made over $100,000 in a given year, plus some endorse-

ment money for wearing a certain type of visor. Joe LaCava has admitted that he earned over $200,000 in eleven months caddying for Fred Couples when Fred was winning everything in sight, and Bruce Edwards has had several years in which he's earned in the six-figures.

I pay Mike eight hundred dollars a week, plus eight percent of what I make, so if I win $15,000, he'll make $2,000 for the week. If I win the tournament, he gets ten percent. (I hope that jibes with the figures Mike turned into the IRS. If not, I guess I'll see him again the next time they hold the San Quentin Invitational.)

Anyway, Mike's happy with the arrangement, and that's important, because I need to know there are at least two people at each tournament pulling for me—him and me.

While I'm thinking about it, let me say I feel the Tour has always treated caddies miserably, and there's no excuse for it. Until recently, caddies never had a good place to eat at the tournaments. Players could take relatives or friends who were caddying for them on a particular week into the buffet lines, but regular Tour caddies were relegated to the barnyard. Lately, Joe Grillo, a former caddy nicknamed Gypsy, has taken to driving a big chuckwagon from stop to stop, and preparing hot food for the caddies. It's called the Caddy Wagon, and I find myself eating there about three times a week. It's a great retreat from the congested clubhouse scene.

I hope this treatment of caddies as second-class citizens ends in the near future, because the Tour should acknowledge their importance to the whole business of professional golf. As a whole they're a good group of guys, with a strong sense of loyalty to one another that goes beyond color or ethnic origin or regional ties. It takes a new caddy about a year to gain the trust and respect of the other caddies, but once he does he has friends for life.

Despite some inequities, the whole economic situation has improved dramatically for caddies, and as I said, those who pack for winners can have lifelong careers. Guys like Mike Hicks, who caddied for Payne Stewart, and Mike Carrick, who caddies for Tom Kite, may have started originally just to travel for a year or two and see the Tour up-close before they planned on getting a "real" job. But they've done so well as caddies that they could never go back to conventional employment without taking a serious pay cut.

Besides helping me in all the obvious ways on the golf course—carrying the bag, reading greens, giving yardages—a caddy can also be extremely helpful by directing traffic around the course and functioning as a personal marshal. Mike can ask for quiet when I'm over a shot, and help clear out spectators when I drive it into the rough. A caddy is also the only security guard a player has around the course.

I generally like to get to the driving range about an hour before I play. I'll hit balls for about thirty minutes, chip and putt for twenty to twenty-five minutes, then get to the first tee about five minutes before my starting time, so I can properly introduce myself to the first-tee announcer and his assistant, and the lady scorers and volunteers, and the kid carrying the standard. (You especially want to make an impression on the lady scorer so she can cheat for you and help you have better statistics in the Greens-in-Regulation and Driving Distance categories.)

The hour before I tee off is pretty much all business, and Mike helps me keep my mind on the upcoming round. Autographs are something I sign only after my round is over. I'm happy to sign them at that point, but I just won't do it before I play, because it costs me valuable practice time and causes me to lose my focus on the task at hand. This policy occasionally causes hard feelings.

In 1988, a fifteen-year-old boy who was watching the PGA Championship at Edmond, Oklahoma, had apparently asked me for an autograph as I was walking to the driving range, and I had told him I couldn't sign until after the round. That fall in school, he wrote a paper for an English class in which he said Peter Jacobsen had been one of his idols, but I had proven to be just another prima donna athlete because I had refused to sign his autograph book.

His parents sent me the essay, and although they were apologetic about it, they thought I should see it. I wrote the boy back and explained that I had my own rules and regulations to follow. It worked out okay, because he got a letter *and* an autograph, but it's an example of how you can hurt people's feelings without meaning to.

Another time, Mike had to physically step between me and a man who was angry with me for not signing his book. It was at the Tournament of Champions at LaCosta in 1991, and he was standing by the locker room door as I walked out. He had a book full of golf trading cards. It looked like he had every card from every sport in there, including the Honus Wagner original and the Mantle rookie card and the Billy Ripken four-letter-word card. Anyway, he asked me to sign, and I said what I always do, that I couldn't right then, but that if he'd catch me after the round I'd be happy to.

He said, "Everybody else has signed for me."

I replied, "Well, I make it a rule for myself not to sign anything before I play," and walked on.

He said, "How come? What's so special about you?"

I turned back to the guy and said, "Look, I didn't fly all the way to San Diego to sign your cards. I came here to win this tournament, and if you can't understand what I'm trying to tell you, then fine."

Then he got real nasty. He said, "Why don't you appreciate the fans? It's the fans who pay your bills."

This debate was obviously not going to be settled with a handshake and a pat on the shoulder, so Mike interceded and pushed me out the door and toward the driving range. He knew if this kept up I'd either shoot 79 or score a technical knockout.

The point is, professional golfers are not like baseball or football players. We don't have somebody hauling our luggage for us, we don't take a team bus to and from the field of competition, and we don't have a shroud of security into and out of the stadium. We're pretty vulnerable out there, and an aggressive fan or spectator can pose a threat.

The plus side is that by not being owned by anybody, I can't get benched, or put on waivers, or optioned to the Durham Bulls.

As I've implied, if there's one thing Mike likes better than golf, it's the Grateful Dead. When we got to the Bank of Boston tournament a few years ago, Mike informed me that the Dead were playing just up the road in Providence, Rhode Island. Although he'd already been to about fifty of their concerts in the previous twelve months, he announced he was going and said it was way past time that I caught their act. Not having a good excuse to turn him down, I decided I better see what the fuss was all about.

I threw on a pair of khaki jeans and a blue denim workshirt with the sleeves rolled up and put on my Nikes. It was about as casual as I could get with my limited traveling wardrobe. A pullover sweater and golf slacks just weren't going to cut it in that crowd. When Mike came to pick me up, he was wearing a Grateful Dead T-shirt and slip-on moccasins with socks. I was thinking he'd be better off without the socks, but then, Mike's not exactly a slave to fashion. And under the circumstances I was in no position to criticize.

I figured that I'd be identified as a charter member of the Geek Patrol once we got there, but what the hell. Maybe there was a Certified Yuppie section I could sit in. Hoping to allay my fears, I asked Mike if I would be the squarest-looking guy at the concert, and he just gave me that sly smile of his that means "Yes" multiplied by a thousand.

When we got to Providence, there were police barricades set up all over the place and a mob of people in the street. It looked like there was some sort of protest march going on, but it was actually just the Deadheads mingling around before the concert. Everyone was wearing tie-dyed T-shirts, and tie-dyed pajama bottoms, or at least tie-dyed headbands with ponytails sticking out.

I felt like the guy in *Quantum Leap,* as though I'd been time-warped back to the late 1960s and dropped on the corner of Haight-Ashbury in San Francisco. Many of the people were about forty or forty-five years old, but it looked like they'd hung onto their college wardrobes. Even the little kids with their parents were dressed in hippie chic.

It was an interesting role reversal for the two of us, because no one knew me from Adam, and everyone knew Mike. Men and women alike were shouting his name, and he was nodding and waving at everyone. These were fellow Deadheads that he'd met along the concert trail, and they were like a big family. Very few of them had any idea that Mike Cowan was a Tour caddy; they just knew he hung out with the Dead. They also probably wondered who the Nerd was tagging along with him.

Inside the concert hall, the communal atmosphere was even more pronounced. The music at Dead concerts is piped into the hallways and refreshment areas, and in all parts of the arena people were dancing around with their arms waving, tracing invisible patterns in the air. There was also a distinct aroma pervading everything that smelled sort of like Bermuda grass without the Bermuda. And it seemed to be making everyone quite happy.

I walked around a while just to soak up the atmosphere, and when I returned and sat down, a startling thing happened; an extremely heavyset girl seated next to me put her hand on my leg and started rubbing it. Her hand had been on the armrest, but it casually slipped off, landed just above my knee, and stayed there. Then the fingers started moving. I kind of twitched my leg to shake her free, but the hand held its position. Now when I say this girl was heavyset, I'm trying to be nice. The fact is, she looked like Refrigerator Perry's big sister.

I could tell that Mike saw it, but he didn't say anything. He just kept smiling. So I whispered to him, "Mike, do you suppose she thinks her hand is on her *own* leg?" I actually wondered whether her legs were so big that maybe she had lost the feeling on the outer edges. I realized it was a crazy notion, but the girl never once looked at me or gave me any other signals. Still, there was no denying the fact that her hand had attached itself to my leg like a land crab, and it was heading for deep sand.

Finally, Mike couldn't hold it any longer. "She recognized you," he said. "When you were gone, she told me she was a *big* Peter Jacobsen fan, and she wants to know if we want to go to a party later."

"Big is right," I said. "C'mon, we're leaving now." And we split. Hey, I'm a happily married guy, and even if I weren't, I would have purchased the girl a Richard Simmons "Sweatin' to the Oldies" video long before I would have squired her to a party of Deadheads!

The recognition count for the entire evening was: Mike Cowan, 327 fans; Peter Jacobsen, 1. At least I didn't pitch a shutout.

And my caddy and I had a lot more to talk about the next day than the speed of the greens.

Great caddy stories abound on the PGA Tour, but I do have a couple of favorites:

—A few years ago, Adolphus Hull, known as Golf Ball, was caddying for Raymond Floyd at Memphis. Golf Ball is one of the best veteran caddies around, but on more than a few occasions he's had trouble finding his way back to his motel at night. Anyway, through the first four holes of the opening round, Raymond had missed every green, a couple long and couple short. As usual, he had made a bunch of difficult up-and-down saves for par, and going to the fifth hole, he was even-par.

He hit a big drive, and Golf Ball gave him a yardage to the green. Ray took out a seven-iron and flushed it twenty yards over the green. He couldn't believe his eyes. He'd been hitting everything perfectly, and he'd just missed his fifth green in a row.

He grabbed the yardage book from Golf Ball and looked at the fifth hole diagram, which bore no resemblance to the hole they were playing.

"What the hell book you got here?" he said. "Is this the book for Memphis?"

And Golf Ball's eyes grew wide. "Memphis?" he

shouted. "Are we in *Memphis*? . . . I thought we were in Fort Worth!"

As if having the wrong yardage book weren't enough, Golf Ball threw gasoline on the fire when they climbed into the bushes over the green and, with Raymond fuming over a nearly impossible recovery shot, said, "Now get this one up and down for me, podnaw."

—This story could be called "A Downer for Upper." Five or six years ago, a popular caddy named D. J. (Father) Murphy, who passed away last year, was caddying for Brett Upper in the AT&T Pro-Am at Cypress Point. On the famous 16th hole, Brett hit his tee-shot long left over the green, down onto the beach. The ball usually goes in the ocean there, but when they got to the edge and looked over, there it was sitting up nicely in the sand. He took a wedge and went down to hit it. Meanwhile, Father Murphy stood by the green to give Brett a general direction. Brett got over the shot and was all set to hit it, when Murph yelled at him to hold up. It seems one of the amateurs, who was well out of Upper's vision, was getting ready to hit a chip shot.

As Brett politely waited for the amateur, with his back to the ocean, a big wave suddenly came crashing in and drenched him up to the chest. He was absolutely soaked. As if that weren't bad enough, the wave washed the ball out to sea, so Brett had to slosh back to dry land and take a penalty for a lateral water hazard. Needless to say, he was not a happy camper.

And one other thing: Brett had teed off on the back nine first, so it was only his seventh hole of the day. I wonder which hole his socks dried out on.

CHAPTER 9

Showbiz

As SOMBER AS the PGA Tour may seem at times, it still exists primarily for entertainment. Despite the large QUIET paddles fans are always having shoved in their faces when players are trying to hit shots, we do want them to have a good time at the course. And if golf tournaments weren't televised, and corporate America didn't feel it could reach a lot of consumers with its products, the million-dollar purses we play for each week would be cut in half.

Although it may be difficult for a touring pro to think of golf as entertainment when he's lipping out three-footers or bouncing balls off condos, part of being a professional is not letting your own troubles ruin the enjoyment of the fan who's paid money to see you play. The bottom line is that it's a business for us players, but an entertainment for the fans, and the more we can blend the two the better off the sport will be.

I've always tried to acknowledge the showbiz aspect of golf, and I feel a responsibility to do all I can to show the public that golfers can be fun-loving and entertaining. This has caused me to risk making an ass of myself at times, but what the heck. If I were deathly afraid of embarrassment, I'd never be able to put a ball on a tee in front of a big crowd.

I don't mind doing something outrageous if it'll help break the unfair stereotype of Tour-player-as-robot. An example was my infamous *Golf* magazine centerfold in 1983. Not surprisingly, it was CBS announcer Gary McCord who first came up with the idea of spoofing the fashion layouts the women professionals did each year in *Golf*. They have always been tastefully done, primarily to promote the femininity of the lady pros, and while there has been lively debate surrounding the marketing strategies employed by the LPGA, most men and women golfers alike really enjoy the pictures.

Many of the women who have posed for these photos, such as Jan Stephenson, Cathy Reynolds, Kris Tschetter, Laura Baugh, and Cindy Figg-Currier, are friends of mine, and they all look terrific in the layouts. McCord's idea was not to put the women down, but to play a joke on the men and show how basically untanned and unattractive we look when we take our clothes off.

We ended up with Keith Fergus, Greg Norman, Payne Stewart, Rex Caldwell, and yours truly. Obviously, there was no intention of using flattering lighting or air-brushing or anything to disguise the fact that we were basically un-buffed guys with weird tan lines. Our forearms were brown, and that little V at the neck was brown, and all other body parts were "A Whiter Shade of Pale." Greg Norman's lucky his nickname wasn't changed from Shark to Albacore, because that perfectly described his coloring in the pictures.

The photo editors at *Golf* got very excited about this project, which was shot in the locker room at the Players

Championship in Jacksonville. They had all the pictures mapped out—Greg in the shower, Payne shaving, Keith in the sauna, Rex toweling off—and they'd gone out and purchased this awful-looking tight underwear that accentuated every bulge. The sad fact is that professional golfers tend to have a lot of bulges in the rear and sides and not much where it counts. Our sport does not require rippling abdomens or popping veins or calves shaped like bowling pins. The only vein that pops on my body is in the middle of my forehead, when a birdie putt does a 180-degree lipout.

On the other hand, we can hit five-irons farther than the longest drives of the last three Mr. Olympia winners.

Everything about the layout was a lark. The first picture was of us standing in the locker room, with a foot up on a bench. The attitude we were supposed to project was something like: "Here we are, we've just finished our round of golf, we've stripped down to our bulge-hugging red Speedos, and we're ready for a hot night on the town." Yeah, sure.

Our actual plans after the session were to rush back to our hotels, order up room service, and watch *F-Troop* on the cable channel. What a joke! But we just smiled and yukked it up and wondered whether we'd be able to live through the heat we'd take from the other players.

Somehow, I got selected for the centerfold, probably because they figured I had the highest threshold of humiliation, or maybe because they felt I was the most decadent. Anyway, they laid me over a bench and draped a big towel with *Golf Magazine* printed on it over my mid-section. What a waste of linen! A ball-washer hankie would have been sufficient to preserve my modesty and ensure that I wouldn't expose the old rut-iron.

The layout was copied from *Playboy,* complete with the

"Golfmate Data Sheet" with all my vital statistics and personal comments. My "Turn-ons" were: big galleries, small scores, long drives, short rough, fat paychecks, and skinny trees. My "Turn-offs" were: water hazards, players whose swings I couldn't copy, three-putts, and four-putts.

When the pictorial appeared, the reaction was ninety percent positive. Nearly all readers realized we were just poking fun at ourselves. Of course, there are always a few that catch you by surprise. A couple of readers thought none of this had been done tongue-in-cheek (if you'll pardon the expression). They said stuff like, "What are you doing? These guys have got terrible bodies, and they've got bad tan lines."

To which our reaction was, "Well, no shit!"

And naturally there were the feminists who thought we were having a joke at the expense of the women golfers. Jan Stephenson—who's taken a little grief from feminists herself—was asked about the layout, and said, "Well, it just goes to show what we've been saying all along. That all the good-looking professional golfers are on the ladies' tour." Her response was right on, and it was exactly what we had had in mind when the project was conceived.

I also got a surprising reaction from a long-time Portland friend, who had moved away a few years back. He wrote a letter attacking me from a Christian standpoint, citing several verses from the Bible about the immorality of it all. I get the feeling he missed the point, too.

I guess it's just like golf: every shot makes someone happy, and someone else unhappy. And that's the way it was with my "beefcake" shot in *Golf* magazine.

Another "showbiz" opportunity came along in 1987, when I was offered a small part in the HBO movie *Dead*

Solid Perfect. The film was based on Dan Jenkins' novel of the same name, and tells the story of an also-ran on the PGA Tour who somehow manages to overcome a mangled personal life and win the U.S. Open. Jenkins is one of my favorite writers, and his book was hilarious, so when Dan and the director, Bobby Roth, offered me the chance to play myself as a guy who beats Randy Quaid's character in the Colonial Invitational, I couldn't resist. (I had beaten Payne Stewart in a playoff to win the Colonial in 1984, so I knew for sure I could handle Randy Quaid.)

Ben Crenshaw had been originally slated to play the part, but Ben got cold feet after he read the script, which contained a fair amount of spicy language, and a little nudity. Crenshaw has that image as Gentle Ben, you know, so when he decided to pull out, the obvious choice was Dirty Peter, the decadent slut who had posed for a nearly nude centerfold. I was secretly disappointed when they told me they didn't want me for my body after all, and in fact would prefer it if I kept all my clothes *on* during the entire filming of my part.

They paid me $10,000 for one full day's work, and they gave me a Screen Actors Guild card, so it was actually a pretty good deal. They also relied on me for technical advice, to make certain the golf scenes looked authentic. I thought that would be the easiest part of the job. It turned out to be the toughest.

Bobby Roth had said to me, "Now, Peter, keep your eyes out for anything that doesn't look right. And give me the benefit of all your experience so that these scenes will have total credibility with golfers."

Well, in my first scene, in which we were being announced on the first tee at Colonial, I noticed that Randy's caddy—an actor named Larry—was standing there with the bag on his shoulder. Larry obviously had not done a lot of looping in his climb to screen stardom. I walked over to him and said politely, "Larry, you wouldn't be holding the bag while we're still on the tee. You'd have it standing on the ground in front of you, with your hands on the head covers or on the sides of the bag."

He ignored me and turned to Roth, and said, "You're the director. You're the only one I take direction from."

Bobby then repeated what I had just said, so Larry took the bag off his shoulder and set it on the ground. It was obvious I needed to be more assertive in my new role as a Hollywood technical advisor.

We played along, and did several takes hitting each shot, and I thought to myself, "Hey, what's so tough about Hollywood? You get as many mulligans as you need to get it right."

I couldn't help thinking how nice it would be in actual tournaments if every time I hit a bad shot I could drop another ball and say, "Take two. Roll 'em."

Shoot, if you gave me just five mulligans a year on the PGA Tour, at exactly the right spots, I could play my way into the Hall of Fame. And so could a hundred other guys.

But I must say I was impressed with Randy Quaid's golf game. On most takes, his first shot was more than acceptable. In fact, when they announced us on the first tee that day, he ripped a beautiful drive down the middle about 250 yards. When we shot a second and third and fourth take, he did the same thing. The guy really showed me something. He was also just great to work with, as were Jack Warden and most of the other people I met that day.

My friend John Rhodes, a teaching pro at Colonial, caddied for me in those scenes, and whenever the camera crew was setting up for another shot—which was often—

John would work with Randy on his swing. It really shows in the final product. Believe me, there are worse swings than Randy Quaid's in professional golf.

I hope the movie came off as being authentic in the golf scenes, but as I said, it wasn't without some effort. In one scene around the second green, Randy is in the left bunker, the pin is on the right, I'm on the back left of the green lining up a putt, and Randy has to blast a shot all the way across the green to the hole. As they were preparing to roll film, I looked over, and my pal Larry was standing in the bunker with the bag. I walked over and said, "Larry, you wouldn't be standing in the bunker. You'd be off to the side holding the rake."

Larry turned away, just like one of my daughters does when she's mad at me for making her turn down her boom box as it's blasting that creative new rap music that we've all come to love.

So Roth went over and once again repeated what I'd just said, and Larry grumpily removed himself from the bunker. The amazing thing is that when I saw the final cut of the film, I thought Larry did a convincing job as the caddy. I guess it speaks for him as an actor, because in real life I swear he didn't know an embedded ball from a hole-in-one.

My favorite scene in the movie is when Randy's character comes back to the motel room after a miserable day in a tournament resembling the AT&T National Pro-Am at Pebble Beach. His wife, played by Kathryn Harrold, asks him what he shot.

He says, "I shot a seventy-f——five."

She says, "Oh, I'm sorry. By the way, honey, I saw a deer today." And she looks up at him with an expression of awe and wonder at the beauty of nature.

He comes totally unhinged, and tells her and the deer

and the world in general that they can go f—— themselves. Granted it's a harsh scene, but every golfer who's ever played the game seriously can understand this volcanic eruption. I just hope I've never been so consumed by my golf game that I've done that to Jan, although she could probably tell you a few stories if you asked her.

On second thought, don't ask her.

While we're on the subject of movies, one of my great frustrations is that I've been unable to secure the movie rights to my favorite book, *Golf in the Kingdom*. Ever since reading it in 1984, and then having that first-round lead at St. Andrews, I've been talking the book up, and my enthusiasm has infected Jack Lemmon as well.

Jack sees himself producing the film and playing the role of Seamus MacDuff. We've talked to Sean Connery, another true golf aficionado, and he's expressed interest in playing Shivas Irons. Should we ever be able to put the deal together, I'd be more than willing to take a hiatus from the Tour for several months for the chance to play the part of Michael, though I've never made that a contingency of the deal. I just want to have some say in the making of a story that really gets to the core of the game I love so much.

For those who feel I'm being foolish in thinking I could pull off the acting job, remember what I learned from my brief involvement with *Dead Solid Perfect*. In Hollywood, they get a bunch of mulligans if they don't get it right the first time. That's a luxury I don't have when performing my impersonations in front of thousands of people, or doing a television broadcasting stint for millions, or playing a sidehill three-iron to the final green tied for the lead. And it's not as if the role is really a stretch for me. Michael is a fellow on a quest to understand the meaning of golf and how the game fits into the big picture. Heck, I've been on that quest all my life.

Whether I ever play Michael or not, I know the part has to be played by an excellent golfer. I don't want a situation like the one in *Follow the Sun,* the movie of Ben Hogan's life. Although I liked that film very much, every time Glenn Ford, portraying Hogan, set up to make a swing, the camera cut away to the real Ben Hogan hitting the ball. The viewer is jolted out of the illusion and reminded that he's only watching a movie, and I don't want that to happen to *Golf in the Kingdom.*

I started looking into the rights as soon as I got back to the States after the British Open in 1984, and eventually called Michael Murphy himself. Over the last several years, we've had many wonderful conversations, and I've become somewhat of a disciple for *GITK* and Murphy's other books, including *The Psychic Side of Sports.* For various reasons, though, I've never been able to get those movie rights.

My quest goes on to this day, however, and while I'm probably too old now to play Michael, I'm not worried. With every passing year, Jack Lemmon and Sean Connery become even more appropriate to play Shivas and Seamus.

CHAPTER 10

Learning About Celebrity

As you gain notoriety in any highly visible arena, be it golf, music, or films, there comes a time when you have to show a face to the public. My role models in this regard have been Palmer and Lemmon. They've been stars nearly all their lives, and yet they never show the strain of their celebrity. They simply have a way of making the fans who approach them feel special.

Arnold is the best I've ever seen at signing autographs, or going out of his way to smile when he's frowning inside. On many occasions, I've seen him finish a round disappointingly, maybe by hitting a poor iron-shot to the final green or missing a makeable birdie putt. But he'll immediately shake it off and sign autographs for twenty minutes. Believe me, when you finish poorly you'd rather chew the scorecard—and the pencil—than sign autographs. It's Arnold's generosity with his fans that has, above all, made him the most popular golfer in the history of the sport. Palmer understands that the fans don't care how he played the last hole or the round, they just want to have contact with him.

Jack is also cordial and giving, almost to a fault. As hard as Jack works at playing his best golf when we're grinding it out in the AT&T National Pro-Am, he will still stop along the fairway and pose for a picture, or take the time to chat with fans who've come out to the course to cheer him on. I've said many times, if Jack and I could play that tournament in a soundproof booth, with no one around, I'm convinced we'd win it. But that's one of the prices of fame, and Jack Lemmon gladly pays it each time he's in the public eye.

If these two guys, with their level of celebrity, can take the time to show respect and kindness to their fans, then I certainly can do the same.

I won't deny that it's very flattering to have people point you out. When I first started playing the Tour, I was disappointed when fans didn't recognize me as a professional golfer, but, of course, it was because I hadn't done anything to deserve their recognition. You've got to go to war and show them what you're made of to earn their respect.

When many of the fans did get to know me, they naturally assumed my personality off the course was the same as the one on it, and it created some awkward situations. While I like talking with fans away from competition, and enjoy a good joke as much as the next guy, it's another matter entirely in the heat of battle.

Sometimes people will poke their heads out of a gallery and tell me they went to school with my dad or were a sorority sister of my mother's, and that can really set me on my heels. In any other situation, I'd love to engage them in conversation and ask them questions about their friendship with my parents way back when, but if the comment comes as I'm needing a birdie to make the cut, or am in contention to win a tournament, I have to keep my blinders on and stay focused, even at the risk of being rude.

If professional golfers could educate fans to any one thing, I'll bet it would be this: that playing golf for a living requires tremendous concentration, regardless of what kind of exterior we show. Even the most talkative players, such as Chi Chi Rodriguez, Fuzzy Zoeller, and Lee Trevino—while they're great entertainers and sometimes act as if they're doing standup routines on the course—are actually just letting off steam. That's how those guys handle the anxiety of their profession. When the pros talk to the crowd, a lot of times they don't necessarily want the crowd to talk back to them.

I don't want this to sound harsh, but touring pros in competition should be treated the same as any on-the-job professional making a living. I've known doctors and lawyers who think nothing of approaching me in the middle of a round and chatting away like I've got nothing better to do. How would a surgeon feel if I busted into an operating room when he was doing open-heart surgery, and said, "Hey, Doc! What kind of scalpel are you using today?" Or, "When you stitch him up, are you going to use a conventional knot or a Windsor?"

Obviously, professional golf is not open-heart surgery, but the etiquette of respecting someone's profession should be the same.

I've heard the argument that the fans pay their money, so they should be entitled to scream whatever they want. But there is a difference between a major-league ballpark or basketball arena and a golf course. I mean, Charles Barkley has a guaranteed contract that pays him several million dollars a year, whether he makes that free throw or not; and Jose Canseco can go zero for twenty-four, as he did in 1992, and still get paid in gold bullion on the first of the month. If Peter Jacobsen misses four cuts in a row, he gets zero, zed, zipperino. There are no guarantees in my contract. In fact, I have no contract. Not to mention that Jose gets to wear skin-tight pants that show off his butt, and I have to wear lime-green plaid pants with a thick white belt. It's just not fair.

Lee Trevino has said, "Guarantee *me* three million a year and you can scream, yell, or spit on my ball when I'm putting. Because even if I miss it, I still get paid."

Until that time, I'm certain Super Mex would appreciate your silence when he's sweating over those ten-footers.

Let me repeat: in the proper setting, I love talking to fans, especially about topics *other* than golf—because I'm not certain there's a whole lot they can tell me about golf that I don't already know. My least favorite conversation is one in which a fella insists on giving me a shot-by-shot description of his most recent round.

When a guy starts out with a line such as, "On number one, I pulled out my trusty Big Bertha and hit this pretty fade . . . ," I have a stock comeback. I'll put my hand on the guy's shoulder and say, "Excuse me, Harold, but can I ask you a question?"

And he'll say, "Uh-h, sure."

And I'll say, "Are we going all eighteen holes today? Because if we are, I'm going back to the clubhouse and rent a cart."

Ideally, at this point I can get him laughing and be spared a fifteen-minute verbal excursion of his 93 with six one-putts. That's one reason I'm glad they televise our rounds on Tour: it saves me a lot of explaining.

There can be awkward moments with fans even off the golf course. One in particular I'll never forget.

I was in Palm Springs with the family for the Bob Hope Desert Classic, and my oldest daughter Amy was just three or four at the time. We were walking out of a Kentucky Fried Chicken outlet with a bucket of wings—extra crispy, I believe—when an older couple, walking in, recognized me. Now, when you're with a little one, as any parent will tell you, you have to hang onto their hand at all times in public, but I was caught in the middle of holding Colonel Sanders in one hand and opening the door with the other, when this woman said, "Say, you're Peter Jacobsen. How are you?"

I said, "I'm fine, thanks."

She said, "What did you shoot today?"

Meanwhile, it happened in a flash. Amy bolted out the door onto a side street of Highway 111, which is the main drag in Palm Springs. She was about four steps into the street when a car came barreling about forty miles an hour right at her. It was a dark street and the driver was not paying attention.

I had one eye on this woman and one on Amy, and just as I was in mid-sentence, I screamed, "Amy!"

Thank God, she stopped stone-cold in her tracks. The car whizzed by her and I know the driver never saw her, because he didn't even touch his brakes. He missed her by no more than three feet. She would have been killed for sure.

I ran to her and grabbed her and was near tears, because I had almost let my inattention allow my child to be run over. It had been nobody's fault except mine, because the woman was just trying to be friendly. I was still shaking when I got back to the hotel and told Jan what had happened.

When I'm out with the family now, people will approach for autographs or to chat, and I honestly enjoy that.

But no one can detain me for long, because Kristen will remind me that she's hungry for pizza or Mickey will inform me that we're late for *Ernest Goes to Camp* or *Pee-Wee's Big Adventure*.

Priorities. They're the stuff of life.

I had my own close encounter with a celebrity years ago, with unexpected consequences. It was at a 1980 press luncheon for Muhammad Ali in Montreal. I was up there for the Canadian Open. The announcer was introducing all the dignitaries in the crowd, and finally he looked over at a side table and said, "And from *Saturday Night Live,* Mr. Bill Murray, and from *Rolling Stone* magazine, Dr. Hunter S. Thompson." Murray was in the middle of filming *Where the Buffalo Roam,* Thompson's "life" story.

I'll never forget the sight. Those two characters were sipping Wild Turkey through straws from a large ice bucket, with their feet up on the table. I snuck over to their table and introduced myself. I loved Murray's comedy so much I had to do it. Bill and I hit it off right away.

Some years later, at the U.S. Open at Shinnecock Hills, Bill and his brother, Brian Doyle-Murray, came out to watch me play. It was Thursday afternoon, I'd just completed the round and had given my caddy, Mike, the afternoon off. I was in the locker room with Bill, just putting some stuff away. Shinnecock is an old club and the locker area is very small. Many of the players had their golf bags lined up in front of their lockers. I decided to go to the range to hit some balls, so I said to Bill, "C'mon, grab my bag. You are now my caddy."

Immediately, he dropped his lower lip and went into his Carl the Greenskeeper impersonation from *Caddyshack*. "Yes, sir," he said, "I will be right along."

He picked up my golf bag and swung around, and inadvertently created a domino effect which knocked over the two bags standing next to mine, belonging to Hale Irwin and Barry Jaeckel. While the normal person would have been embarrassed to death, Murray immediately went into his improvisational comedy mode and started intentionally knocking over bags. He'd swing around and knock over a bag, swing the other way and knock over another one. All the time, he kept apologizing as though they were people. "Oh, excuse me, Mr. Palmer. Oh, please forgive me, Mr. Nicklaus." Suddenly, I was watching a *Saturday Night Live* skit.

About four or five other guys were in the locker room eating lunch and they were all doubled over laughing. Then Murray went into a nerdy trot out the back door, with the bill of his cap turned backwards, his pants hiked up over his belly button, and the bag swinging all over the place.

Curtis Strange was just walking into the locker room as Bill flew past him, and Curtis' eyes became like saucers. He put his back to the wall, and said, "Whoa, let me get out of this guy's way." I could tell from his expression that Curtis was wondering how I'd ever hooked up with this guy, and how in the world he had gotten past the USGA Dobermans into the locker room.

We headed over to the driving range, and the first person we saw was Raymond Floyd. I introduced Bill to him, unaware that the swing Raymond was honing right then would lead him to the U.S. Open title just three days later.

This being the Open, security was pretty tight on the range and greater than normal restrictions were in place. Obviously, no one other than the players was allowed to hit practice balls, so we moved to the quieter end of the range, so we could break the rules. After I'd hit a few, I asked Bill if he'd like to show me his action. He didn't hesitate a second. He grabbed my driver and immediately started pumping tee-shots, providing his own commentary as he went.

With the lip jutted firmly out, he'd hit one and describe its flight for the fans: "Ah, it's looking pretty good . . . oh, it's heading for trouble . . . oh, my God, it's found the second cut of rough. The dream has ended."

It didn't take long before players and fans alike started to watch this exhibition, and with the increased attention, Bill really turned it on. A green snow fence was between us and a hospitality tent, where hot dogs and hamburgers were being cooked, and Bill started lobbing wedges in that direction, reenacting the scene in which "Carl" swings a rake in the tulip bed at Bushwood Country Club.

Bill would take several waggles, then lisp, "What an incredible Cinderella story. This unknown comes out of nowhere to lead the U.S. Open at the Dunes at Shinnecock Hills . . . the normally reserved crowd is on its feet for the Cinderella Kid . . . what a difficult up and down . . . I think he's got a wedge."

He took the club back slowly, then lobbed the ball in the direction of the tent. "Oh, he's got to be pleased with that one, it looks like a miraculous . . . it's in the hole!"

Just then, the ball bounced off the top of the tent, and Murray dropped his club and put his hands to his head.

I thought for certain I was going to become the Pete Rose of golf—wrongly banned for life from the Tour.

One time, Bill and I were actually partners in a team competition. It was at Butler National Golf Club, prior to the Western Open; a celebrity shootout had been organized to benefit charities in the Chicago area.

All the celebs were current or former professional athletes, guys such as Michael Jordan, Mike Ditka, Jim McMahon, Walter Payton, Ernie Banks, and Doug Wilson of the Chicago Blackhawks. Murray, a Chicago native from a golfing family, was the only non-athlete, and so, of course, I chose him as my partner so the gallery would pull for us as underdogs.

The format was alternate shot, in which both players hit a drive on each hole, select the better ball, then alternate from that point on.

When we got to the last hole, we were down to just two teams: D. A. Weibring–Michael Jordan vs. The Underdogs. On the 18th, Bill hit a big fade into the 10th fairway, but we had an open shot to the green. The wind started to howl about forty miles an hour and it looked like we might get some lightning, which reminded me of *Caddyshack* again—the priest who plays a perfect round until he's struck dead by lightning on the last green. (I also recalled that it was on this same course that Lee Trevino, Bobby Nichols, and Jerry Heard actually were hit by lightning.)

It seemed appropriate under the conditions that the finish be dramatic, and it was. Bill hit an incredible flop wedge for our third shot, over the front right bunker, and I made a four-foot-par putt to win $10,000 for Bill's designated charity.

All the print and electronic media swarmed around Murray to get his reaction, so naturally he dropped his lip and went into his spiel.

"Finally, I'm vindicated," he said. "I'm certainly one of the most talented athletes ever to come out of the Chicago area, and I've been largely unappreciated. People like George Halas and the Wrigley Family and Ditka and Payton have kept me down all these years, but at last I'm able to claim the glory that is rightly mine. I am now recognized as a true athletic hero . . ." And on he rambled in a frenzied state for five minutes.

It was wonderful for the event, and the charity, to have Murray steal the moment. And I remember just standing back watching him, with a big smile on my face, thinking, Damn, I love this game.

That same week I played a practice round with Michael Jordan and became aware of just how big a star he was. I guess I'd been unaware of it before because Michael is so down-to-earth. He's not one of those bow-down-and-kiss-my-ring type of guys, with an entourage of yes-men always around him. He talks to everybody in the same manner.

I had bumped into Michael in an equipment van earlier in the week, while he was getting his grips changed and having the lie and loft on his irons checked. It started to rain, and he was really disappointed.

"Man, I was hoping to hit some balls this afternoon," he said.

So I asked him if he wanted to play with us the next morning.

He said, "Sure, but you better okay it with Mr. de Young."

Peter de Young, the Western Open tournament director, said he thought it would be okay. The next morning, at eight A.M., Michael teed off with Ben Crenshaw, Chip Beck, and myself. By the time we reached the third hole, word had spread that Air Jordan was on the course, and our gallery had gone from around twelve people to twelve hundred.

About then, a PGA Tour official approached me and

said, "Peter, you know you can't do this. This is highly irregular and against Tour policy."

Which it was. Only the contestants playing in the tournament are allowed to play practice rounds. I had asked Michael to play, however, and I wasn't about to tell the world's most famous athlete that he had to pack it in. Besides, the gallery was having a great time. So I asked the official what the fine would be, although I knew from my position on the Tour Policy Board that it would probably be about a thousand dollars. The official said, "I don't know, but I'm probably going to have to write you up."

"I understand," I said. "That's your job, and I'll pay the fine. But the people out here are having a great time, and that's more important than the fine."

I wasn't crazy about the idea of paying a thousand dollars in greens fees for Michael, but I was in no position to argue.

To his credit, the official never did write me up. He even came up to me later and said, "It was really great to see him out there. Everybody was lovin' it."

It goes to show that with someone as special as Michael Jordan, even the PGA Tour can bend the rules a bit. The Tour is, after all, show business.

I got a greater sense of how Jordan is worshipped in Chicago when I teased him on national television during the 1992 NBA Finals between the Chicago Bulls and the Trailblazers. When Chicago was in Portland for Games three, four, and five, I invited Michael to play golf at The Oregon Golf Club, the new course that I had co-designed. We played eighteen holes one day, and the next night he had his normal, brilliant game.

The Oregon Golf Club is a difficult course, rated at 75, and that day Michael shot 85 from the tips of the back tees:

46 on the front nine, and 39 on the back, highlighted by an eagle on the par-five 13th hole. That night at the game, I was pulling hard, as always, for the Blazers, and Ahmad Rashad, who'd played football at the University of Oregon and whom I'd known for years, saw me and told me he was going to ask me on camera about playing golf with Michael.

Sure enough, in the third quarter, with the Blazers making a run and the crowd screaming so loud I could barely hear my own voice, we went on the air, and Ahmad said something like, "We all know Michael Jordan wants to be a championship golfer, and here's a real championship golfer who played with Michael yesterday. Peter Jacobsen."

I was standing there trying to guess what Ahmad was going to ask me in front of thirty million Michael Jordan fans. He said, "Peter, Michael really wants to play the Tour. When do you think he'll be good enough to go out there?"

Well, with Michael being the star of the Bulls, and my being a diehard Blazer fan, I had to dig him a little. So I said, tongue in cheek, "I'll be playing center for the Bulls before Michael plays on the Tour."

And then I reported what Michael had shot that day, and I added that I thought he was a very good player, with a lot of potential.

The next day, the Associated Press ran a blurb on my comments in every newspaper in the country, and the post-game talk shows in Chicago made a big issue of the fact that I had criticized Michael's golf.

Peter de Young called me the next morning from Chicago, and said, "Boy, do they hate you back here!" I had to remind myself how tough it is to poke fun at things that people consider sacred—and believe me, in Chicago, nothing is more sacred than Michael Jordan.

Let me just say here and now—so I don't further alienate the Chicago fans—that Michael could surprise a lot of people. He hits the ball long and has probably the best coordination I've ever seen. But there's a lot more to it than that.

No contemporary athlete has made the transition from super-stardom in one sport to success in golf, with the sole exception of John Brodie. But unlike Jordan, Brodie was hardly a latecomer. He'd been a competitive golfer since he was a little kid, a scratch player in college at Stanford, and even took a brief fling at the regular Tour during the off-season when he was in the National Football League.

Michael would have to spend the next fifteen years after his basketball days ended totally focused on improving his golf game, and playing in good competition, to get ready for the Senior Tour. The odds would still be long—but if anyone could ever pull off such a feat, it's probably Michael.

Long ago, when he was cut from his junior high school basketball team, I'm sure no one thought he would become one of the most admired basketball players of all time, either.

Chapter 11

The Politics of the Tour

Now that I've mentioned my position on the Tour Policy Board, this is a good occasion to get a few things off my chest.

Although I occasionally enjoy public speaking and like to debate a good issue, the closest I'll ever get to politics is my service on the Board. While it's an elected position, there's no campaigning allowed. You can't stump for the job, or make Willie Horton commercials, or hire a private investigator to take pictures of other candidates kicking their ball in the rough. You just agree to have your name put on the ballot, and then submit to a vote of the other players. My first term lasted from 1983 to 1985, and my current term is through 1993.

There are nine members on the board: three Independent Directors, representing the public interest; two PGA Directors, who are national officers of the PGA of America; and four Player Directors—myself, Jeff Sluman, Brad Faxon, and Rick Fehr. Together, we oversee all the marketing, television dealings, promotions, finances, policies, and rules that govern the activity of the Tour and its players.

We meet four times a year, for a day and a half each, and there's never enough time to address all the issues. It's often a no-win proposition, too, because all the players on the Tour are independent businessmen used to running their own show and getting their own way. Their opinions run all over the place, and a decision for the collective good always means that there are individuals opposed—and that the Player Directors will hear from them.

A few years ago, for instance, some players were opposed to having R. J. Reynolds as a corporate sponsor, because they felt it implied the Tour was advertising a cancer-causing product. No action was taken on it, and they felt their opinions had fallen on deaf ears. Nothing could have been further from the truth, but for a while, the Player Directors were looked at suspiciously, instead of as the allies that they are.

I know I base all my votes on what would be good for the future of the Tour rather than what would be good for me individually, and the other players on the Board do the same. There's no compensation or reward for serving—it's just a way to give something back to the game.

There's also been some controversy around the role of the Commissioner. The Tour Commissioner is appointed by the Policy Board to be chief executive and administrative officer of the PGA Tour, and while Commissioner Deane Beman attends all our meetings, and offers important input, he is directed by, and works for, the Board. Some people feel Beman tells the Player Directors what to say—some call us Deane's Dopes or Deane's Clones—but that just isn't the case. And anybody who knows me can tell you: *nobody* puts words in *my* mouth.

While Beman exhibits a great knowledge of business, he sometimes falls short at public relations. He definitely could use more PR types around, so that the lines of communication with the media and the players would be more open and less susceptible to hearsay and rumor. I also believe more needs to be done to generate support for the tournament directors and the corporate sponsors, because they are the lifeblood of the Tour.

Overall, however, I think he's been good for the Tour. He's kept it organized, kept it moving forward, and deserves credit for engineering the tremendous increase in prize money. He's also been a driving force in the growth of the Senior PGA Tour and the Ben Hogan—now the Nike—Tour.

Having said all that, several issues still need to be studied further, and here goes:

I believe the current rule that exempts from qualifying the previous year's top 125 money-winners, is wrong. I'd like to see the number reduced to 90 or 100 at the most. It's an unpopular position to take, but I liked the old system, which exempted only 60 players each year and which changed in 1982.

Obviously, the old Monday qualifying that was held each week was a nightmare for the Tour's field staff to operate, and it was tough on scheduling—but it was eminently fair for all the players, because it gave everyone who had earned a Tour card the chance to play each week. It also really taught you how to play golf under pressure. Guys such as Tom Watson, Tom Kite, Lanny Wadkins, Calvin Peete, Bruce Lietzke, John Cook, Hale Irwin, Craig Stadler, and Chip Beck all learned to be great competitors by climbing their way up through the Top-60 system.

The only thing that rankled me was that everyone called those who weren't in the Top-60 "rabbits." The term implied that the non-exempt players just lived on the fringes of the Tour, nibbling from week to week on any lettuce that had slipped off the table where the big boys dined. Well, if that was the case, they should have just called it the PGA Rabbit Tour, because at least three-quarters of us had to face Monday qualifying from time to time.

Once you got into a tournament, and then made the cut, you were exempt for the next tournament, so streaks of good play were rewarded. Conversely, a missed cut sent you back to square one. There were times when I played seven or eight weeks in a row if I was making the cuts, even if I was brain-dead, because if I skipped a tournament I defaulted my exemption and it was back to Monday qualifying.

At the beginning of each year on the West Coast, for tournaments such as Tucson and Phoenix, there were often only one or two spots available on Monday, so I'd go out knowing I had to shoot a course record to get in. That was pretty tough. But later in the year there were always plenty of spots available, and I usually had a good idea before I teed off what it would take to qualify.

Knowing that 70 or 71 is the magic number will force you to learn course management: whether to lay up or go for it on par-fives, whether to shoot for middles of greens or dead at the flags. There's no question those Monday qualifiers either broke you or made you stronger than tempered steel. Those of us who survived the "rabbit era" are much better players for it today, I'll guarantee.

Under the current system, which exempts as many as 150 to 160 players from a variety of categories, a player can float from week to week and month to month without feeling any serious pressure. It may be the main reason the Tour went for the latter half of the 1980s without any individual domination.

I'm not advocating a return to Monday qualifying, because Mondays have become a valuable source of revenue to players who've earned the privilege of doing special outings around the country. These exhibitions also expose the stars of the Tour to regions of the country that don't host regular Tour stops, and thus enhance the popularity of our sport. I just think we need to look at lowering the number of exemptions.

Oddly enough, these thoughts come following a season when I finished 126th on the official money list, one spot below the cutoff of totally exempt players, so my thoughts are obviously not tied to my own situation. (My status for 1993 is as a conditionally exempt player. Fields are filled currently in the following way: top 125 on the previous year's money list and tournament winners within the last two seasons, top-ten money winners of the 1992 Ben Hogan Tour, top 40 qualifiers from the 1992 qualifying school, then numbers 126–150 off the 1992 money list. With my current position, and hopefully a few sponsors' exemptions, I should still play a full schedule of 25 tournaments this year.)

Quite simply, I need to play better this year, and am more determined than ever to do so. In a game in which you have to let your clubs do the talking, my clubs barely spoke in a whisper in 1992.

As Chip Beck said to me as we played together in the last regular event of the year, the H.E.B. Texas Open, "Pain and suffering are inevitable in our lives, but misery is an option." Chip's right on the money.

What I've learned from the experience is that I have to work harder, stay more focused, and fight my way back to where I feel I belong. If we all look to ourselves for improvement, rather than looking for handouts, we'll keep the American Tour the world's most elite showcase of golf. And that's in the best interest of all the players.

I also have strong feelings about the Tournament Players Clubs. The idea of stadium golf, in which courses are designed to give greater accessibility to the fans and provide unrestricted views of tee-shots, fairway shots, and putts, is a tremendous innovation. The master plan went awry, however, when so many of the TPCs were designed as target golf courses. All those railroad ties, and the humps and bumps in the greens that sometimes cause good shots to bounce over the boards into water hazards, are an absolute joke.

The original idea was that each TPC course would be designed by a well-known architect, who would be assisted by a Tour player functioning as a consultant (in some cases, two players). The theory was that the consultant would offer playability suggestions so that the final result would be liked by the people who actually had to use it, but it didn't work out—simply because the architects had wax in their ears.

Time after time, the guys on the Tour would hate the new TPC courses, and blame the player/consultant, who would say, "Look, I suggested this or that, but the architect didn't listen to me."

And then the sportswriters would fuel the controversy

by writing about the prima donna players on the Tour crying about their own golf courses. But the fact was, they *were* poorly designed. They didn't reward creativity, they were predictable in their sameness, they weren't fair, and they weren't fun.

When I won the Sammy Davis Jr.-Greater Hartford Open in 1984, I was openly critical of the TPC of Connecticut course at Cromwell, which had been redesigned from a traditional Scottish-type course into a target golf course.

In the press conference, I said I was thrilled to win the tournament because of the great tradition of the event and Sammy Davis' long-time involvement, and because of the wonderful people of Hartford, who were as supportive as any golf fans in the country. But I questioned the redesign of the back nine. I didn't like it at all. And then, throwing diplomacy to the wind, I listed all the reasons why.

Gordon White, a writer with *The New York Times,* told me after the press conference that it was the first time he'd ever heard a pro win a golf tournament and then criticize the course.

Fortunately, we've softened the design of many of these abominable target courses, and most of the TPCs are now much improved over the first go-round. That includes the course in Cromwell, Connecticut, which is now excellent. A decade from now, I think target golf will be looked back on as the disco music of golf course architecture. We'll simply laugh and wonder how we could ever have been so light-headed.

I hope the architects we select from now on will put those railroad ties where the sun doesn't shine and return to the wonderful traditions established by men like Donald Ross, Dr. Alister Mackenzie, and A. W. Tillinghast.

We don't need to reinvent the way golf is played. It's been a pretty darned good sport all along.

Another area in which the Board needs to become much more aggressive is the problem of slow play. It's gotten progressively worse through my years on the Tour, and we never do much more than talk about it. We were talking about it during my first term in 1983, and we're still talking about it today.

The increase in prize money is certainly a factor. Because players realize the importance of every shot, they take as much time as they can to avoid making errors of judgment.

I'd guess the average round on Tour these days is four hours and thirty minutes when we play threesomes, and three hours and forty minutes when we play twosomes. It's not uncommon for us to play the first hole, and then wait ten minutes on the second tee. We then play the second hole, and wait five or ten minutes on the third tee. It's ridiculous how bad it's gotten, yet the Tour has gotten away from the two-shot penalty for slow play. The only penalty in recent years is a piddling fine of five hundred or a thousand dollars, and I can't remember the last time a fine was levied. Besides, one thousand dollars doesn't exactly strike fear in your heart when you're playing for top prizes of $180,000 or more each week.

The two-shot penalty would be far more effective than a small fine, because if you're in contention and are warned about slow play, you know two shots could cost you a victory and all the perks that go with it.

The Tour has come up with a pace-per-hole formula for monitoring play, but it hasn't worked, and it's too hard to police, anyway. None of the tournament officials likes putting a stopwatch on the players. Besides, our officials are too valuable as rules experts to be wasting their time as speed cops.

We ought to institute the simple practice of keeping up with the group in front of you. It's the way I was taught to play by my father, and it's still the best rule of thumb. If your group falls more than a hole behind, it should be given one warning, and if it doesn't catch up quickly, all players should be given a two-shot penalty. Believe me, peer pressure within a threesome will take hold if one player is dragging his feet.

It would also help if the Tour went back to the practice of "ready golf," as opposed to "who's away?" It's something we do when a player has to change his shoes at the turn, or use the facilities, so why not do it all the time? If *we* did it, the golfing public would follow suit and play would speed up all over the country.

I also think too many Tour players waste time around the greens by not lining up their putts until it's their turn. At least ten minutes can be saved during each round if players were more time-efficient around the greens. Maybe the Tour should just do a video of Lanny Wadkins and Jim Gallagher, Jr., playing three holes on a normal day, and give it as a model to each player who makes it through the Qualifying School. That might solve the entire problem.

While I'm striding around on that soapbox, I believe certain existing restrictions on Tour players need to be reviewed and revised. The first of these deals with a player's right to appear on television. Basically, when you join the PGA Tour, you turn over your rights to play golf on television to the Tour's discretion. This can be unfairly restrictive at times.

Let's say I want to have three fellow Tour players join me on a weekend when we're not competing to have a memorial tournament honoring my father. And let's say all proceeds will go to junior golf or cancer research or the Muscular Dystrophy Association. Additionally, a local television station wants to broadcast the event. Well, I can't do it because it's against the by-laws of the Tour to play in any other event from Wednesday to Sunday when a Tour event is being played.

A tournament like our Fred Meyer Challenge is okay under this rule, because it's played on Monday and Tuesday. But it's hardly cheap. This year we'll have to pay the PGA Tour $140,000 for the right to have our tournament televised on ESPN.

Basically, the Policy Board has decided that to protect the PGA Tour's ability to get on TV and to negotiate the proper rights fees, they have to prevent an influx of golf tournaments from being televised. The irony is that many of these events are developed by their own players, such as Jack Nicklaus Productions, and Greg Norman's fun event of a few years ago, which pitted him against Wayne Gretzky, Ivan Lendl, and Larry Bird.

While I understand the Tour wanting to prohibit the flooding of the market, I believe more golf on TV builds a greater interest in the game. After all, people watch an event on television because it excites them, not just because it's a PGA Tour event. Evidence of this is the long-running success of the *CBS Golf Classic* and *Shell's Wonderful World of Golf*.

Another area I find restrictive is the PGA Tour's ability to prevent a player from competing overseas. There's an unwritten rule of thumb: you get to compete in one overseas tournament for every five regular Tour events in which you play. If you play in the required fifteen tournaments, you're allowed three overseas events. But there are inconsistencies in the way these approvals are given by the PGA Tour. Some players have never asked for a release in their long careers on the Tour, and when they do request one the first time, even if it's for a non-televised one-day pro-am, they're sometimes turned down. On the flip side, some highly successful major-championship winners get released for four or five overseas tournaments, a few above the limit. And some of the big boys don't ask at all and still go!

Put simply, the control of these releases is inconsistent, unfairly preferential, and shouldn't exist at all. All our players are proud members of the PGA Tour and would never do anything intentionally to hurt it or its future marketability.

While you may see a Fred Couples go overseas and receive tremendous appearance fees to play—as much as $150,000 for a single tournament—Fred also knows where his bread is buttered, and that's on the PGA Tour. Couples would not abuse the privilege if there were greater flexibility, because he knows those appearance fees exist primarily because of his Top Dog status in America. If he slips down the money list in the U.S., there are plenty of guys anxious to jump into his spot, and then the overseas guarantees would be there for those players, and Fred would have to work his way back up.

If anything, Couples' appearances in Europe improve the marketability of the PGA Tour over there, much as the Dream Team's participation in the Barcelona Olympics enhanced the worldwide stature of the National Basketball Association.

The fact is that the various world tours, be they men's

or women's or seniors', revolve around the three American tours. While the European Tour has grown stronger, and is doing very well, it still falls behind the U.S. Tour in the number of good players, and in the organization of the whole show. The PGA Tour is the undisputed jewel, and I think the Commissioner has to show more faith in the judgment of our players to do what's right.

The bottom line is that it is the players in any sport who make it popular, not the administration.

I also have a few thoughts about the four major championships—those special tournaments that draw all the fanfare and are the most valid gauge of determining greatness. Each of the majors has its own unique identity, with one exception—and I think that can be rectified.

Let's start with the Masters. For tradition, beauty, and excitement, it's in a class by itself. It's the only major played on the same course each year, which gives it a sense of nostalgia and history unrivaled by the others. It's also the greatest offensive show in golf: there's no rough, the par-fives are all reachable, and the back nine is eminently dramatic, from Amen Corner to two par-fives where both eagles and double bogeys are possible. The electricity in the air on Sunday is unmatched in all of golf.

If the Masters is an offensive show, the U.S. Open is the greatest defensive test in golf. This was demonstrated by Tom Kite's win at Pebble Beach, in which every par felt like a victory. The winds were howling, the greens were like linoleum floors, and the rough felt as if you were walking through a burial ground for sheepdogs. There was no moisture at all on the course—each blade of grass had cotton-mouth—so the ball would not stop on the greens, which meant you were scrambling for par on every hole.

And that's precisely what the USGA has in mind—to make par a precious figure. I don't have a problem with that. It's their show, and that's fine.

The third major, the British Open, is totally different. It's played on a rotation of seven seaside links, magnificently natural courses with no trickery. No one tries to grow rough; they take whatever is there. There are huge sand dunes, and hardly any grass on the fairways, much less the greens. It's totally un–American, which I think is great, because it demands more creativity. The British and Scottish courses bring bump-and-run and the art of chipping back into golf for the ugly American.

Ken Venturi told me he goes to Ireland for two weeks each year so he can learn to play golf again. After playing so much target golf in America, he said, he almost forgets that the ball is round and was meant to roll on the ground.

The best thing about the fourth major, the PGA, is that it offers forty spots to PGA club professionals, who are the backbone of golf in this country. Those fellows teach the game and sell the game to the average fan who comes out to watch the Tour, and they do much more to promote the sport of golf than the Tour players. For them, the PGA is a chance to prove to their club members that they can play good golf, as well as administer all the other responsibilities of their job.

However, the PGA Championship needs to be rethought, because at present it is the only major tournament with no individuality in its course set-up. It's perceived as a U.S. Open–wannabe. The PGA sets up golf courses just as the Open does, with baked-out greens and pet-cemetery rough.

It's actually very simple to practice for the U.S. Open and the PGA, because you know if you miss the green you have only one or two shots to play: a blast out of a bunker,

or a lob wedge that you hack out of long grass. A player
may have an arsenal of different chip shots, but he won't
need them for these two tournaments.

David Feherty editorialized on this very issue in *Golf
World* magazine shortly after last year's PGA. In describing
how you must hit a shot out of abominable rough around
the greens, David wrote: "You're reduced to a hundred-
yard swing with your buttocks clamped at 2,500 psi, hoping that the recipient of the venomous swipe doesn't fly
out like a wounded snipe across the green straight into the
very same crap." How funny. How true.

I'd suggest the PGA let the USGA have the patent on
rough around the greens, and by mowing the fringes bring
back the craft of pitching and chipping. It will be more fun
for the players and more interesting for the fans.

In addition, both the Open and the PGA often go to a
great course and then dishonor it by making changes, such
as turning a medium-length par-five into a 480-yard par-
four, or doing something unusual that essentially alters its
nature. I would argue that if you select a great course to
host your tournament, you should respect its greatness.
Making those changes is like hosting an art show and
saying, "For this special show, we're going to turn Leo-
nardo Da Vinci's *Last Supper* into a Texas barbecue, and
add one arm to the Venus de Milo, so she can embellish the
product of our corporate sponsor, Rolex."

While I do understand that technology changes through
the years and that the golf ball does go farther, these courses
are masterpieces and shouldn't be tampered with.

I would also recommend they rethink the way the fairways are cut at the PGA. At Bellerive in 1992, and in most
PGAs, they usually have 26 to 30 yards of fairway, and just
one mower-cut (four to five feet) of perimeter rough,
before you get to the cabbage. This isn't the best way to do

it, because a straight driver who mis-hits his tee ball a little bit will jump and roll easily through the perimeter rough and then stop one foot into the cabbage—with no shot. Meanwhile, a wilder driver, who missed the fairway by twenty yards right or left where the gallery's been walking, will often land in tromped-down grass and have an easier shot. I'd suggest cutting the fairways slightly narrower, then having maybe eight to ten yards of perimeter rough on either side. You'd still have the same general width of playable grass, but the straighter driver won't be penalized as much as the wild one.

Finally, I'd suggest that the PGA Championship go back to being played on national treasures that haven't been seen in a while, rather than on so many new courses, as has been the trend in recent years.

I just don't think a tournament with such a long history and tradition of its own wants to be thought of as *U.S. Open: The Sequel.*

CHAPTER 12

Bringin' 'Em Home

ALL THESE SUBJECTS I've been expounding on became of even more interest to me in the last few years, because I took on some new challenges: I helped start a tournament and co-designed a golf course.

My desire to bring the stars of the PGA Tour back to my hometown had its roots in the old Portland Open. My first memory of that event was as an eight-year-old kid, standing in a downpour on the driving range at Portland Golf Club with my dad.

We were watching a large man with a crewcut hit golf balls, and no one else was around. I remember Dad was totally immersed in studying this golfer's technique, and the fact we were getting drenched didn't bother him in the least. I wasn't nearly as interested and started to cry. It was a Saturday and I wanted to get home and watch *Flipper* and *The Jetsons*.

I guess the large man heard my whimpering, because he stopped practicing and came over and held an umbrella over our heads. He said something to Dad like, "Looks as though you've got somebody here who doesn't want to be here."

The man and my dad chatted for a while, and then Dad finally gave in and took his snot-nosed kid home.

I would learn later that the golfer who had been so considerate was Jack Nicklaus. He was in his rookie year, a season which would see him win the U.S. Open and—wouldn't you know it—the Portland Open. When you're eight years old, you're not easily impressed.

Two other golfing events in my youth had a big impact on me. In 1969, Portland Golf Club hosted the Alcan Golfer of the Year tournament. I was then fifteen, and golf had long since surpassed cartoons as my favorite passion. Neither rain, nor sleet, nor dark of night would keep me from watching the world's best golfers in my backyard.

I remember the Alcan had an incredible finish that year. Billy Casper birdied the last four holes and came from six shots behind to nip Lee Trevino by one for the title. Trevino hit an eight-iron into the bunker on number 17, left it in there a couple of times, and made a triple-bogey six. First prize was $55,000, the richest in golf, and second dropped all the way down to $15,000. I also remember Trevino joking and being gracious despite what was probably the worst collapse of his career.

Then in 1970, the U.S. Amateur was held at Waverley Country Club, my home course, and I worked on the greens crew. My job was to oversee several holes and make certain the bunkers were raked and all divots were replaced. Lanny Wadkins made a 25-footer on the 72nd hole to edge Tom Kite by one shot. An eighteen-year-old phenom named Ben Crenshaw, whom I was anxious to watch play, had to withdraw due to a bad back.

During my college years and early years on the Tour, I regretted that the people of my home state no longer had the opportunity to witness up close the best golfers in the world. I resolved that if an opportunity ever came up to do something about it, I would. That time came in 1986.

Mike Stoll, a Portland businessman, and I conceived the idea of having an event that would do just that. At first I thought the only possibility was a one-day, Monday pro-am, but Stoll wisely talked me into a 36-hole two-day event. The two keys to making it happen were getting Arnold Palmer to agree to play (which drew several other top players), and the willingness of the Fred Meyer Corporation and their CEO, Mr. Oran B. Robertson, to sponsor the tournament. The Fred Meyer Challenge was born.

It's been extremely gratifying over the last seven years to know that I had something to do with exposing Oregon golf fans, and especially the young golfers of the area, to the same level of talent I watched growing up. It's also been great to see the wonderful spirit and cooperation of the more than 1,500 volunteers and my staff people at Peter Jacobsen Productions who run the event so beautifully each year. Most gratifying of all is that we've raised over $2.75 million for Portland-area charities.

Several of the traditions that are now so much a part of the Fred Meyer Challenge began that first year, such as the Monday night party. It's a big affair for about 1,500 people, and it's a chance for the contestants and other guests to let their hair down. While we may attend a number of so-called "parties" as professional golfers, we wanted to have a party in the true sense of the word—we wanted people to talk about what a great time they had for days afterward.

That first year we held a charity auction, which happened by accident. One of the premier items was Arnold's sportcoat, which was forcefully snatched from him by our aggressive auctioneers, Curtis Strange, Fuzzy Zoeller, and Greg Norman. They ended up getting a huge price for the coat—a few thousand dollars—and it just spiralled from there. Fuzzy eventually auctioned his own coat, then his tie, then his shirt. By the end of the evening, he was dancing topless to the cheers of the crowd. The last I heard, Chippendale's talent scouts had not made him an offer.

Fuzzy's skin-show started a trend that culminated in our wildest party ever, in 1989. That was the year Curtis was coaxed into violating about sixteen Oregon state blue laws. I was onstage with Arnold and Greg and Curtis and we had made several thousand dollars auctioning off garments, when some lady from the middle of the room yelled out, "The heck with the coats, I'll pay $5,000 for Curtis' jeans!"

Strange understandably protested, but we weren't about to ignore five grand for a local children's charity. Curtis had had a couple beverages, as we all had, and there was an embarrassed grin on his face. The reigning U.S. Open champion really didn't want to take off his 501 button-fly Levis in public, but what with the headlocks and cajoling, we finally persuaded him. He went backstage, and moments later walked back out with his jeans in his hand. All he had on was his grabbers, with his shirt-tail out to around mid-thigh of his bare legs.

When the woman who made the offer saw this, she shrieked and came tripping up to the stage like she'd just been told to Come on Down at *The Price Is Right*. She was panting furiously and her hands were flapping around her head like she'd been attacked by African bees.

Peter Bonanni, the publisher of *Golf* magazine, was seated at a front table with two of my tournament staff, Eddy Ellis and Jim Whittemore, and Peter said, "I just hope no one has a camera here, because every one of those guys onstage is a playing editor for us."

Eddy said, "I'd say *playing* editors describes them perfectly."

We also started a tradition of close, exciting finishes that first year. There were just four teams in 1986, competing in a stroke/match-play format. The team shooting the better score won the match. Curtis and I were partners and we beat Zoeller and Fred Couples that first day, and were paired in the finals against Norman and Gary Player, who had beaten Palmer and Tom Watson. We had a one-shot lead going to the par-five 18th hole at Portland Golf Club, but we played the hole poorly. Curtis made six and I was left with an eight-footer to save par. But Norman and Player also had problems. Greg was fifty feet from the hole in three. It was just two weeks before that I had seen him lose to Bob Tway's bunker shot in the PGA, so I yelled to him, "Tway stole one from you. Why don't you steal one from us and knock this in?" To my amazement, he did.

He got a huge ovation, then Curtis turned to me and laughed, "Now look what you've talked yourself into. You've got to make that to tie."

Although that eight-footer meant absolutely nothing to the world of golf, it sure did to me. For the first time since turning professional, I was playing in front of my hometown. Fortunately, I shook that baby in, and we declared the two teams co-champions.

Another dream was realized in 1992 when we completed the construction of the Oregon Golf Club, a course I co-designed with Ken Kavanaugh. It became the new home site of the Fred Meyer Challenge, primarily because my long-term goal is to bring either the U.S. Open or PGA Championship to our city, and that would never have happened at Portland Golf Club, a wonderful course that isn't big enough to accommodate an event of that magnitude. All of our design features at the Oregon Golf Club—from the golf course to parking facilities, clubhouse, and practice areas—were done with the express purpose of some day hosting a major. With the Fred Meyer Challenge played there annually now, the course will become familiar to the Tour's best players, and to the whole country on national television.

As my youthful interest in playing golf developed, so did my fascination with the artistry of golf course design. I used to make drawings of golf holes during class at Ainsworth Grade School. Later, at Lincoln High School, I would make aerial maps of all eighteen holes and then give the courses unusual names, such as Anchovie Country Club, or Skunk's Breath Municipal. Then I'd hang the drawings in my bedroom and study them, to see how they might be improved.

Coincidentally, the kid who sat next to me in home room in grade school was also preoccupied with illustrations. His drawings were of people, in particular his family, which included his father Homer and his sister Lisa. His own character he called Bart, a variation of Brat, which rhymed with his first name. He called them the Simpsons, and his name was Matt Groening. I wonder what ever became of him?

Although Matt was far more introverted than I, we got along very well, because we both had a slightly twisted view of life. Maybe it's all the rain in Portland. Anyway, I'm hopeful that some day Bart Simpson will become the official trademark of the Challenge, much like Snoopy is for the AT&T Pebble Beach National Pro-Am. (Note to Matt: if you're reading this, call me—collect. We need to do lunch.)

I'm like all golf course designers in that my design tendencies reflect my personality, and my likes and dislikes. I think a golf ball should roll to its natural stopping point, and not always be interrupted by sand traps and water hazards. I therefore employed a minimum of adjoining hazards at The Oregon Golf Club. Most sand traps aren't hazards in the truest sense of the word. Traps usually provide a much easier shot than the player would have had if the ball had kept rolling. Tour players today are so proficient out of sand that they love to see an errant shot go in a trap. It's about two out of three that they'll get it up and down.

When we designed The Oregon Golf Club, I wanted to employ the natural slopes on a hilly piece of property. I tried to leave runways off the sides of the greens, so that a hard-running iron shot, poorly struck, would not be saved by a sand trap but would roll down an embankment, leaving a challenging chip shot.

I wanted the course to reward strategic golf and pay dividends to a player with a good touch. Like tennis or Ping-Pong or billiards, golf should require a lot of feel, so that the force with which you strike the ball determines its outcome. I also wanted to make creative chipping a requisite to scoring well. I was not surprised at all that the first players to win the Fred Meyer Challenge at its new home were good ball-strikers and course-managers, Tom Kite and Billy Andrade. Two other players who fit the same mold, Corey Pavin and Steve Pate, finished second.

The greens were extremely fast—twelve on the Stimpmeter—but they were fair. The players liked the fact that we didn't trick them up with big humps and mounds. Steve Elkington appreciated that they had a minimum of slope, and Pavin said, "Those were some of the best greens we've seen all year. Augusta National's are the only ones comparable." The players were very gracious and most felt the course could be a suitable site one day for a major championship.

I gained a great respect for golf course architects from my work on The Oregon Golf Club. There's so much involved that doesn't meet the eye, from studying topographical maps to solving drainage and engineering problems. It's incredibly time-consuming.

I currently have two other designs under way, Genoa Lakes GC in northern Nevada, and Creekside Golf Club in Salem, Oregon. I'd like to do more if the situation is right, but again only as a pastime. My principal goal continues to be playing as well as I can on the PGA Tour, and, as always, having fun along the way.

CHAPTER 13

Breaking Out of the Mold

"FUN ALONG THE WAY" is as good a way as any to introduce the subject of a certain infamous rock band, beloved by millions around the world. I'm speaking, of course, of Jake Trout and the Flounders.

Who? Let me explain.

I've been a music lover all my life. I enjoy just about every type of music, from country to blues to rock and roll, and my favorites include a pretty wide spectrum: Bruce Hornsby, Huey Lewis, Bonnie Raitt, Jethro Tull, Genesis, Ivan Neville, Dan Fogelberg, and Elton John. I even pick at a guitar occasionally, but I'm about a fifteen-handicap on the strings, and that's with mulligans.

One of my favorites growing up was Alice Cooper, who was as outrageous a rocker as you'll find. He painted his face and dressed weird and did all sorts of grotesque things when he performed, so it should come as no surprise that his favorite hobby is golf. One of these days I hope to play in a pro-am with Alice, whose real name is Vincent Furnier, just to tell him how much I liked his music.

My being a fan of his demonstrates that kids can enjoy rock music without carrying it any farther, because I've never been really big on wearing mascara and eye-liner. I think too often parents use rock music as a scapegoat for their children's problems, but I'll withhold further opinion on that until I become Brother Peter and open a television ministry and theme park with a toll-free 800 number.

When I would mess around with a guitar as a kid, I naturally dreamed of one day being a rock-and-roll star, and my friends and I toyed with the idea of forming a band. With all of our attention focused on girls and golf, however, we just never found the time.

Oddly enough, it was the PGA Tour that finally gave me the opportunity to rock out in front of an audience. In 1987, Commissioner Beman approached Larry Rinker, who plays a mean guitar, and asked him if he could provide some entertainment for the annual players' family clambake at the Players Championship at Sawgrass. Larry asked me if I would get involved and we also talked to Mark Lye (another guitarist) and Payne Stewart, who's a killer on the harmonica.

Larry had some musician friends in Jacksonville, including a keyboardist and a drummer, and we all practiced together outside one of the banquet halls in the lobby of the Marriott at Sawgrass.

Obviously, we couldn't get too sophisticated, so we stuck to two songs that everyone knew—"Twist and Shout" and "La Bamba." We rephrased the words to "La Bamba" to use the names of the Spanish players on the Tour. So the main chorus went "Na-na-na-na Lee Tre-vee-no," and then we strung in the names of Chi Chi Rodriguez and Eduardo

Romero and Ernie Gonzalez. It was every bit as ridiculous as it sounds here, but we knew if we hammered it up enough we could pull it off. And we did.

I was designated as the lead singer, probably because I was the least proficient musician, and because I had the highest embarrassment threshold. I could also come closest to being on key, whatever key we were in. Anyway, we wore sun glasses and put our collars up and tried to fantasize that we were a real rock-and-roll band. The crowd of about 200 players, families, and officials took it in the right vein and really got into it. They stood up and cheered us, and several of the kids circled the stage and clapped their hands, and we had a blast. I thought about ripping off my shirt and doing a flying Wallenda trapeze dive into the crowd, à la Jim Morrison, but two things held me back: my love handles.

While our impromptu concert was good family entertainment, the same can't be said for the way we got our name. People often call me Jake, and Curt and Tom Byrum suggested that since a "peter" is actually a one-eyed trouser trout, I should be christened Jake Trout. John Cook also deserves some credit (blame?) for my stage name.

Mark Lye was looking up definitions in the dictionary one day, and trying to find something "fishy" that tied in with golf. He discovered that a flounder was not only a flatfish of the families Bothidae and Pleuronectidae, but an intransitive verb that meant "to proceed clumsily and in confusion." Obviously, this was the perfect name for our group. So there you have it, the heretofore untold story behind the naming of the best—and only—rock-and-roll band ever comprised of PGA Tour professionals. (I'll bet you're sorry you were ever curious.)

Later on, Rinker suggested we put some music down on tape, so we went over to his house and recorded some stuff with John Inman, who is a good piano player. Naturally, we thought it sounded pretty good for a bunch of amateurs. We were sort of like beginners at golf, who after a round tend to remember the good shots more than the bad ones. Everything about the recording that stunk, we just ignored.

A few months later, we had another jam session at the Buick Open in Flint, Michigan. Danny Briggs played drums, and Willie Wood and Scott Verplank were also there. It was then that we realized that we couldn't get too serious about this stuff. It wasn't as if I could stand up there and croon "Let It Be" or "Bridge Over Troubled Waters" and expect people to be moved to tears—unless it was tears of pain. We couldn't harmonize like the Temptations or move and groove onstage like Archie Bell and the Drells. We were, after all, just a bunch of vagabonds who wore polyester pants for a living. So we decided that if we were going to do this as a hobby, we had to make it funny, and we had to tie it to golf.

Mark Lye and I started taking popular songs and messing around with the lyrics so they'd pertain to our profession. We worked independently at first, then together, sort of a poor man's version of Lennon and McCartney. No, poor doesn't get it. More like destitute.

Mark re-penned "Cocaine" by J. J. Cale to be "Slow Play."

"When you're in a rush, nothin' bothers you as much as Slow Play . . . Don't let it happen today, I gotta catch me a plane, Slow Play . . . We don't like, we don't like, we don't like . . . Slow Play."

Next Mark did "Square Grooves are Goin' " to the tune of Warren Zevon's "Werewolves of London," a play on the square-groove controversy that has dogged the game of golf these past four years.

Then, over at the Kapalua International in Hawaii, I was hanging out at the beach with entertainer Scott Record and we made up the lyrics to "Don't Worry, Keep Swingin'," giving Bobby McFerrin a real run for his money.

"I just saw that shot you hit . . . you're playing so bad you want to quit . . . But don't worry, keep swinging' . . . You just hit your ball into some trouble . . . If you don't chip out, you'll make a double . . . Don't worry, keep swingin'."

Lye had introduced me to two of his good friends, Duck Dunn and Steve Cropper, both of whom play with Booker T and the MGs, and played with The Blues Brothers. Duck and Steve are nuts about golf, and they agreed to perform with us. Shortly after that, I rewrote the great Otis Redding song "Sittin' on the Dock of the Bay," which had been co-written by Cropper. My version was called "Hittin' on the Back of the Range." It went like this:

"Hittin' in the morning sun / I'll be hittin' when the evening comes / Watching all my shots in flight / Knowing I ain't doing it right . . . I'm just hitting on the back of the range / Making a swing that feels so strange / Hitting on the back of the range / Not making a dime.

"I shanked a shot on seven / Chunked a wedge at number nine / three-putted number eleven / I think I'm gonna lose my mind . . . I'm just hitting on the back of the range / trying to be like Curtis Strange / Hitting on the back of the range / Not feeling so fine."

I was relieved that Strange had won the eighteen-hole playoff in the U.S. Open that year, because it's hard to find words that rhyme with Faldo.

When we decided to record all these songs for an album, we did it under out own label, Course Records. Naturally, we had to contact the original artists and music companies to get their permission. My friends Huey Lewis and Bruce

Hornsby, who are golf nuts, enthusiastically gave us the okay. "I Want a New Drug" became "I Want a New Glove," and Hornsby's "Defenders of the Flag" was adapted to "Attackers of the Flags." In fact, when we've attended their concerts from time to time, Bruce and Huey have dedicated songs to us and sung a few of *our* lyrics rather than their own.

But not all musicians we contacted were as gracious. We had changed Randy Newman's "I Love L.A." to "I Love to Play," but apparently Randy didn't want to play, because he turned down our request. I found that surprising, because nearly all of Newman's music consists of parodies anyway, like what we were doing, from "Short People" to "It's Money That Matters." Apparently, Randy is better at dishing it out than taking it.

The other one who snubbed us was Neil Young, whose brother, I had heard, is a golf professional. We had redone his song "This Note's for You," which was a knock on musicians who sell out to corporate America, and written "This Shot's For You." But Neil invoked the stymie rule and proved that he doesn't really have a Heart of Gold.

A friend named John Baruck, who represents several rock acts, including REO Speedwagon and Gino Vanelli, helped us produce the album. John is a great guy and truly a degenerate golfer, because all he wanted for his trouble was free balls and gloves and pro-am tickets, plus an occasional lesson. God bless the barter system.

We recorded at Pegasus Studios in Tallahassee, which is owned by Lye's friend Butch Trucks, the drummer for the Allman Brothers. Butch was also very cooperative, selling us studio time for just a little over his cost. (Butch Trucks helps Jake Trout—sounds a little like a vignette from *Sesame Street*.)

We hired the personnel at Pegasus, and we were backed

by a group of talented Memphis musicians, Ross Rice, Kye Kennedy, and Steve Ebe. All the instrumentals were first class; then they sort of got ruined when I put the vocal tracks over them. But then, nobody would have believed it was us if everything sounded perfect.

If the tape does get your fingers snapping, and isn't too abrasive on the ears, it's because Payne and I did what all true blues musicians do before they record—we got shit-faced. That wasn't our original plan, but when we got to the studio for the big day, and saw all those professionals in there wondering what the hell these two golf bums were doing, we both got nervous. Although it was before noon, Payne said, "Look, I can't do this sober. This is one shot I've never practiced."

It's interesting to consider that here was a guy who could hit a perfect putt to win the PGA or U.S. Open with about twenty million people watching, yet with just a few musicians present, he got the yips with a mouth organ.

Anyway, we made a run to the liquor store in Tallahassee, bought a couple of sixers of Michelob Light, and Payne bought a tin of Red Man. It was the perfect attitude adjustment to prepare for our professional recording debut.

When all the tracks were laid down and post-production had been completed, we came out with just 5,000 copies of the tape. Our expectation level was not very high because we didn't know if we could move even 100 of them. To the surprise of absolutely everyone, however, we've sold nearly 20,000 copies so far. This proves either that P. T. Barnum's line about suckers being born every minute is true, or the damn tape isn't that bad after all. I'd prefer to think the latter.

Certainly part of the tape's success is that everyone out there who watches golf knows that those of us who play the Tour can shoot great scores from time to time, but they want to see the other side of our lives as well. Professional golfers are often criticized for being robot-like, or cookie-cutter impressions of one another, so when we show a more human side, people get interested.

Everyone's seen Payne Stewart striding to victory in his knickers, so it's refreshing to see him in crazy sunglasses getting funky on the harmonica. And Mark Lye, who's sort of a bouncy, energetic guy on the golf course, is a mellow fellow when he's working that guitar. Maybe I'm the least surprising guy in the group, because people expect to see my gums flapping.

Most gratifying of all is when people tell me they bought the tape as a gag, or as a fun gift for another golfer, but then really enjoyed the music when they listened to it.

We got a big publicity boost in the summer of 1989 when former CBS announcer Bob Drum, on his segment "The Drummer's Beat," did a feature on Jake Trout and the Flounders playing at the pro-am party for the Federal Express St. Jude Classic in Memphis. They showed us jamming at the party, and then did interviews with us. I'm glad Drum didn't ask for a percentage of our cassette sales, because it sold like hotcakes after that.

Our biggest gig ever was in Naples, Florida, at a pro-am hosted by Lye and his good buddy Glenn Frey, formerly of the Eagles. Jake Trout and the Flounders played golf during the day and performed outdoors that night in front of 15,000 people on a ticket that included Frey, Jack Mack and the Heart Attack, Vince Gill, and Jimmy Buffet. When we were introduced that night, I'm sure many of the concert-goers probably thought we were hosts of one of the Saturday morning fishing shows on ESPN. But they didn't throw us overboard. In fact, we got a nice ovation.

Curiously enough, on two of the occasions when the Flounders performed, I have had two of my best tournaments. I went on to finish second to Jodie Mudd at Memphis that year, losing by one shot. Then in 1989, we opened the show at Kapalua and did our last three songs with the entire Blues Brothers Band backing us up. Two days later, I won the tournament, beating Steve Pate in a playoff.

I bring up those two occasions because I'm often criticized for getting involved in too many activities, the claim being that these hobbies hurt my golf game. The truth is that my outside interests keep me enthused about golf, and help me to play better. If all I did was play and practice, I might go a little crazy. As much as I love golf, there's a whole lot more to life than fairways and greens.

There is a downside to doing something colorful and fun as a professional golfer, though, and that is when people don't know where to draw the line between my occupation and my hobby. People frequently yell "Hey, Jake Trout!" at me on the golf course, or ask me how I learned to play the harmonica or some other instrument I don't play, or ask when our next album is coming out. If I'm preparing to hit a shot at the time, I have to back off and try to regroup. I know the person is just trying to be friendly, but it's difficult for me, because I can't shift gears that fast.

In response to the next album question, all I can say is that Mark and I have rewritten enough good songs to fill another one, and if time permits, we'll probably do it. I think one of the next songs will be a parody of Pink Floyd's "Another Brick in the Wall." We'll call ours, "Another Nick in the Ball," and dedicate it to all our pro-am partners.

As I mentioned earlier, this desire of mine to break out of the stereotype of the boring touring pro has gotten me into trouble from time to time. I can think of no better example than the stunt I pulled during the final round of

the Western Open at Butler National in 1990. A little
background is in order here.

As you may know, I live in Portland and am an avid fan
of the Portland Trailblazers. I've watched them go from an
expansion team in 1970, to the world championship with
Bill Walton and Maurice Lucas in 1977, through some
more lean years and back to where they're now one of the
top teams in the NBA. As a result, I was very proud that
they made the NBA Finals against the Detroit Pistons in
1990. The championship series was underway the same
week as the Western Open.

Now, some golf fans may also recall that Butler National
had been a bittersweet venue to me the prior two years. In
1988, needing only a par on the 18th hole for an outright
victory, I hit my second shot into the proverbial watery
grave over the green and in the process snatched defeat
from the jaws of victory. As the saying goes, every shot
makes someone happy, and I had caused a little-known
professional named Jim Benepe to become well known
with that shot. Jim not only won the tournament, but
became an exempt player for two years and got all those
nice perks that go to tournament winners, such as invitations to the Masters, Tournament of Champions, and
World Series of Golf.

The next year, 1989, I lost a Monday morning sudden-
death playoff to Mark McCumber. So I had a higher than
normal profile with the Chicago area fans. They viewed
me as something of a tragic figure, sort of a poor man's
King Lear, for lack of a better analogy.

In 1990, I had started the final round of the Western six
strokes behind 54-hole leader Wayne Levi, but I really got
it going and after birdieing numbers 12 and 13, I was six
under par for the day and had moved to second place. I was
still well behind Levi, who was blitzing the field, but I was

looking for my third good finish in three years at Butler.

I decided to have some fun at that point and show the fans and a national television audience where my sympathies rested. I pulled a Portland Trailblazers souvenir jersey out of my golf bag and put it on over my shirt. I then proceeded to birdie the 14th hole, wearing the jersey.

The fans couldn't believe what they were seeing, and I knew the CBS announcers couldn't ignore it in the booth. I was having a blast with it, because I knew my golfing Blazer friends, like Clyde Drexler, Terry Porter and all the Portland faithful, would get a kick of it, and it was just another way of showing the fans that all of us pros have a life outside golf. As I walked down the fairways, I could hear people saying things such as, "What's this guy doing?" or "Go Blazers," or "Go Pistons," or, in one instance, "What a jerk!"

Most of the Chicago fans were polite and supportive, perhaps because they also had practice rooting against the Pistons, who had eliminated their beloved Bulls in the playoffs that year. And after the round, in which I shot 68 and finished third, I got a good-natured ribbing from the media, who understood that what I had done had been in good fun.

It was the next week, at the U.S. Open at Medinah, that a delayed reaction to the jersey incident really blew up in my face.

I've always considered my game well-suited to U.S. Opens, and in fact, of the twelve Opens I've been privileged to play in, I've made eleven cuts. The one cut I missed was that year at Medinah.

The first omen that it wouldn't be my week was when the shaft of my driver snapped on the practice range on Tuesday. I couldn't find a replacement that I trusted, so I played all week using a three-wood off the tee.

That little problem was nothing compared to the reaction I got from the fans. A picture of me wearing the Trailblazer jersey had run in all the Chicago-area newspapers, and the rest of the country had seen it on CBS, so to quote a song from my youth, there was "nowhere to run to, baby, nowhere to hide."

The U.S. Open is different from most tournaments, in that golf fans fly in from all over the country, so it's truly a national gallery. And the folks that had flown in from the various regions all had their favorite NBA teams. These people, I'm here to tell you, were loaded and cocked and ready to fire on me. It was vicious at times, with fans vocally expressing their displeasure with the Blazers, or their support for the San Antonio Spurs or the New Jersey Nets. I mean, the Open is tough enough on your nerves without getting heckled on every hole.

By the time the tournament started, the Trailblazers had lost in the Finals four games to one—including three straight in Portland—so I heard various terms of endearment, such as "The Blazers Suck," "Portland Sucks," "You Suck," "Your Wife and Kids Suck," "Your Dog Sucks."

Come to think of it, we don't have a dog, just two cats.

Anyway, I played the first two rounds with Ian Woosnam and Fred Couples, and Ian turned to me at one point and said, "You know, I thought our English football (soccer) crowds were bad, but this is worse."

I was literally getting barbecued every step of the way. I can only compare it to one of those rides at Disney World, in which each time you pass a certain point, a monster jumps up and startles you. Walking down those fairways at Medinah was an E-ticket on the Jungle Ride. As soon as I'd pass a group of people, they'd feel it was their turn to speak, and they'd jump up and fire away. Obviously, not everyone was demeaning—some were actually cheering me on—but it's the nasty ones you remember at times like that.

In the second round, I was safely under the cut line with three holes to go, but then I bogeyed the 16th and 17th holes. Now I needed a par on number 18, or I would miss my first-ever cut in an Open. I drove into the right rough, but fortunately had a decent lie for my second shot.

When you drive a ball off the fairway, and fans scurry around the ball to get a vantage point to watch your recovery, you are really challenged to maintain your patience and composure. This is where golf is like no other sport.

In basketball, when a player dives for a loose ball, he lands in some pharmacist's lap. Of if he's lucky he lands on a cheerleader. But at least he has the option of getting up quickly and returning to the court.

When you drive into the rough as a Tour player, however, you can't just jump back into the fairway. You have to gather all your powers of concentration to avoid making a big number. This is never easy. Having already hit it into the junk, you're not in a good mood to begin with, and then you have to deal with some of the fans rubbernecking around you, secretly hoping you'll play knock-knock like Woody Woodpecker and make a nine. Others behave as though you've ventured off the fairway for the express purpose of having a conversation with them.

Anyway, I had a four-iron to the green, and I needed to slice it around a tree out of a semi-flyer lie. I knew I had to make par to make the cut, so I was really bearing down. Just as I completed my pre-shot routine and was settling into my stance, some malt-liquor connoisseur yelled, "Hey, where's Kevin Duckworth when you need him? He might move that tree for ya." (Hiccup, burp!)

My thoughts at that time were a million miles from the

Trailblazers and Duckworth, but now I had to back off the shot and wait for people to quit giggling. When I finally hit the ball, it came out slightly fat and short of the green. I pitched poorly and missed my par putt, and all of a sudden I was down the road with an empty load.

Walking to the car after signing my scorecard, I was totally enraged at what had gone on for those two days. Here, I'd tried to do something amusing by donning that jersey—something I'd hoped would give the fans a kick—and it had backfired on me. I remember fuming to Jan, who was walking cautiously behind me, "Boy, I'm never going to show my support for anything again. If they want robots out here, then I'll become one."

About then, as Mike Cowan was putting my clubs in the trunk, a couple of guys walked by and one of them said, "Go, Blazers! They'll get 'em next year."

I didn't even think about the fact that he was trying to say something nice to me, I just knew I'd had it up to my gills with comments about basketball. So I turned and said, "Oh, yeah? Well, f—— you!"

Jan quickly shoved me in the car and said, "I've never heard you talk to anyone like that!" And fortunately, before the guy walked over to retaliate, we peeled out of there.

I didn't sleep much that night because I was angry, embarrassed, confused, and full of self-pity as well. Looking back on it, I hope that fellow I unloaded on will read this book and know I'm sorry. But there's not much chance of that. He probably holds me up there with Don King and Mike Tyson as one of the true gentlemen of sport.

CHAPTER 14

Wired for Sound

THERE'S A BUMPER STICKER that says, "Old golfers never die. They just lose their balls." I certainly hope that's not true, but if it is, thirty years from now I'm going to regroup with Jake Trout and the Flounders and go on the road performing the greatest hits of Little Anthony and the Imperials. I can see it now: a bunch of old farts in plus-fours singing falsetto.

Actually, most professional golfers never retire. They don't call press conferences, as Sugar Ray Leonard did three times, to announce that they're quitting, and they don't have farewell tours like John Havlicek or Kareem Abdul-Jabbar. Old golf pros tend to do one of three things: they go on the Senior Tour or retire to the broadcast booth or become inventors of golf gimmicks guaranteed to shave ten strokes off your game.

I had been asked many times whether I would eventually pursue a career in broadcasting, and with my new agreement with ABC Sports I'm looking forward to doing much more TV work this year, and at the same time playing a full schedule of tournaments. I feel I still have many good years as a player, but then touring pros always think they're just a day away from finding the key to perfect golf. It reminds me, once again, of a scene from *Caddyshack*.

At one point, Murray's character has a pitchfork against a caddy's neck, and he's reflecting on having once "looped for the Lama." But the Dalai Lama was a little slow with payment, so Murray asked him, in his distinctive Carl the Greenskeeper slur, "Hey, Lama. How 'bout, ya know, something for the effort?"

And the Dalai Lama told him he was not going to give him money, but rather on his deathbed Carl would receive Gunga-la-Gunga, or total consciousness.

Eyeballing his captive listener, Murray said, "So I got *that* goin' for me."

One of the advantages to my working with ABC is that the network is giving me the best of both worlds, as an announcer *and* a player. I'm going to enjoy working with Brent Musberger, and I've been encouraged to have fun in the booth. So far, most of the TV work I've done has been as a roving reporter, breathlessly whispering compelling stuff such as, "He's got 178 to the pin, with a little breeze in his face. He's chosen a five-iron."

I've been told in the past that I come off much more conservative as a broadcaster than I do in person. Well, that will change in my new role as a color analyst, but I'm not sure I could totally unwind the way I do when I give a clinic or do impersonations. When people come to watch golfers offer instruction, or to see me mimic swings of the great players, we're the show they're coming to see. When people tune into a golf broadcast, they're certainly not doing so to watch the announcers. The golfers trying to win the tournament are the show. All of the broadcaster's efforts should be toward enhancing the show, but never stealing it.

One of the problems with American telecasts is that there are so many announcers, the director must constantly switch from one to another, so that every thirty seconds we have to hear, "And now out to you, Bill," or "Back to you, Mike," or "Up to you, Fred." It's as if the microphone were a hot potato that no one can hold for long without getting burned. It doesn't necessarily have to be done that way.

I love watching golf broadcasts when I'm in Australia or Europe, because you often have one announcer speaking over a thirty- to forty-minute period covering several holes, and the effect is like a documentary, or a Herbert Warren Wind essay on golf in *The New Yorker*. It's as though you have one voice of reason weaving the story of the day, and if that announcer is good, like Peter Alliss or Alec Hay of the BBC, the viewer has a idyllic experience, much like playing an enjoyable round of golf.

Having been criticized by broadcasters as a player—only to hear the criticism several days later when I'm reviewing the telecast on a VCR—I'm sensitive to the way some analysts get tough on the players. I think an analyst should delve more into a player's mind, and explain what the player's tendencies are under pressure, rather than proclaiming, "That was a bad swing," or "That was a horrible putt," or "I can't believe he hit *that* shot."

Johnny Miller took some flak once for saying I was faced with a perfect opportunity to "choke" when I was hitting my second shot to the final green at the Bob Hope Chrysler Classic in 1990. He referred to the fact that I had a long iron off a slice lie to a green with water all around. Well, he probably could have used a better word than "choke," but he certainly had a point. It was a damn tough shot. Fortunately, I pulled it off and won the tournament, or we might really have something to talk about here.

I must say, though, that, after reviewing the tape, I had a totally different perception of his comment. In context, it sounded as if Johnny was actually trying to protect me from criticism if I did dump it in the drink, because he appreciated just how precarious a shot it was.

Overall, Johnny is an outstanding broadcaster. He's honest, insightful, and funny, and he has absolute credibility with the players because of his great career, in which he faced about every situation a golfer could. He's won tournaments by fourteen shots, and bogeyed the last hole to lose. He's won by coming from way behind (1973 U.S. Open) and while leading the field (Tucson and Phoenix, in 1975) and he's had heart-breaking defeats (the Crosby and at least two Masters come to mind).

Gary McCord's a captivating announcer because he's unpredictable and irreverent, and because he works harder than anyone to get to know the younger players. He can even describe the tendencies of a first-year player who finds himself suddenly leading a tournament. And that's no accident. It's because Gary does more research on players than anyone in the business. He's in the locker room, and on the range, and going to dinner with guys, and basically just working his tail off so he can bring fresh insights to the viewers.

I especially like the "New Breed" segment on CBS, which has been done by both McCord and Jim Nantz. Features which reveal the personalities of the players can only help to humanize them and show that we're not all carbon copies of one another.

People are sometimes surprised at how Gary comes up with all his information. He simply has it stored in a lap-top computer, so if I get in contention and am hitting a shot on-camera, he can call up Peter Jacobsen on the screen and immediately know my likes and dislikes, whether I use an electric razor or a double-edged, what my favorite foods are, what I ate for breakfast, whether I held it down, the whole nine yards.

McCord also uses imaginative descriptions that the audience can understand, but that you appreciate even more if you've played the course. One of my first memories of Gary on the air was his description of a shot at the 16th hole at the Memorial Tournament. Someone had missed the green to the right and the pin was back left. I had played earlier that day and, believe me, the shot he was facing was impossible. Gary said, "Ladies and gentlemen, to illustrate how difficult this shot is, go out into your front yard and chip a ball from your lawn down onto the hood of your car and make it stop. Pretty hard to do, huh? Well, this is tougher."

I laughed and thought, hey, he's absolutely right. And yet I'd never heard a broadcaster say something that off-the-wall. McCord continues to come up with great lines week after week. Putts that lip out have gone over a "cellophane bridge," putts hit too hard have been "nuked," and a player who chunks a pitch shot is said to have splattered Hormel chili all over himself.

Gary's also a much better golfer than he gives himself credit for. In 1992, he won over $60,000 in the first three months, then basically retired to the booth. He also won an event on the Ben Hogan Tour one year by five shots. "They must have been embarrassed that I won," he said, "because they canceled the tournament the next year."

I also appreciate Ken Venturi, because he brings to a

broadcast a reverence for the history of the game and its traditions. And like Johnny Miller, Kenny has been there. I think it's great that Venturi and McCord are on the same network, because between them you get a nice mix of respect for the integrity of the sport, and a more contemporary look at the modern-day player. Their contrasting personalities remind me of the Smothers Brothers. I don't have to tell you which one is Tommy.

As I said, it's important for broadcasters to get to know the players and their tendencies if you're talking about them to a national audience. You want to understand their history of performing under pressure, and discuss each player's mental battle in the last nine holes of a tournament he's in contention to win.

I would also hope that in wearing my analyst's hat at ABC, I would never forget how difficult it is out there. When you're over a shot with a four-iron into a crosswind to a green that runs away from you, and you've got alligators left and pterodactyls right, and you've got to make a birdie to make the cut or win the tournament, your major orifices pucker up, believe me. And it never gets easier, no matter how many years you've been at it.

Part of the challenge of playing on Sunday, when you're in contention to win, is the exorcism of a band of demons that perch on your shoulder and entice you to recall every bad shot you've ever hit in a similar situation. Ideally, you have a few angels on your other shoulder to counter the attack.

As you face a difficult shot, the demons scream, "You aren't that good! You can't pull this off!"

And the angels reply, "You're a Tour player. You had to be good just to get this far. You've hit millions of great shots under pressure. You *can* pull it off!"

And back and forth they go:

"No, you can't."

"Yes, you can."

"No, you can't."

Until you want to scream, "Shut up and let me hit the damn thing!"

I guess when Johnny Miller talks about choking, he means letting the uncertainty in your ability prevent you from swinging naturally through a shot; in other words, giving in to the demons.

But I wish they could come up with another word for it, because it has no similarity to having a piece of prime rib stuck in your throat. Now *that's* choking!

A few broadcasters have a habit that I really hate: they'll approach a player with questions on the driving range as he's preparing to play the final round of a tournament. It's an awkward predicament, especially for a young player, who might not have been in that position before. He doesn't want to turn down the broadcaster, for fear of being thought of as uncooperative, and yet he deserves all that pre-round time to himself, to do whatever he feels is necessary to prepare.

The broadcaster's questioning usually follows this sort of pattern: "Hey, how 'ya doin? Gee, you're playing really well this week. So what are you working on? Who's your teacher? What's the strongest part of your game right now? How will your life change with a victory here? What does it mean to you as a person? Is your family here this week? Are you going to be nervous playing with Curtis Strange and Greg Norman?"

And here's the player hitting short irons to get his muscles in sync, trying to work on up to the driver before he hits a few putts. And he's got this important round to play, and maybe only thirty minutes of practice time remaining, and his concentration gets shattered by someone who should have gotten this information after the previous day's round when the player was unwinding.

I guarantee, now that I'm announcing more, I'll never bother a player in the hour before he plays. A good rule of thumb for broadcasters is the same one often used by players: you better bring your game to the golf course, because you can't count on finding it once you get there.

A pet peeve of my family and the families and friends of all Tour players is: Why on earth don't the networks show more golfers' scores during the telecast? The networks typically show only the first page of the leaderboard, and occasionally a second and a third page, but they'll seldom run through the entire field more than once. NBC does a ten-minute ticker during a football telecast, which shows the scores of all the games, and I believe the audience would be better served if all the networks had a similar feature for golf. Everyone watching has a favorite player or players, and the odds are they aren't on the first page of the leaderboard during a given week. If they ran the scores on a ticker at the bottom of the screen, it wouldn't interrupt the narrative at all.

I do like most of the instruction that's given during a broadcast, especially Venturi's Stroke-Savers, which are concise and not too complicated to understand. I'd actually like to see the networks offer *more* instruction, because the golfing public is growing so rapidly, and golfers are insatiable when it comes to hearing a new tip to improve their games. It might cut down slightly on the number of live shots, but taping significant shots to show one or two minutes later doesn't hamper a telecast at all. Obviously, all the instruction should be slated prior to the last forty-five minutes of air time.

I'd also like to see the players miked more often, as they are each year in the Skins Game. I recognize that it might turn the telecast into an R-rating, but we could start out miking only the fellows who regularly attend the Bible study sessions on Tour, until the rest of us got used to the idea.

And one final item. It would be great if the networks would use natural sound more often. I just love it when there are no announcers talking, and you see a player setting up to his shot, and you hear the crowd in the background, and birds chirping, and the rustle of his clothes, and then the sound the club makes at contact. Natural sound brings the feel of the tournament into a viewer's living room like nothing else.

CHAPTER 15

The Ryder Cup

I'VE BEEN FORTUNATE to be closely involved with two Ryder Cup matches. The first was in 1985, as a member of the American team that played the Europeans at The Belfry in Sutton Coldfield, England. The second was six years later, as a broadcaster for NBC Sports, in the so-called "War on the Shore" at Kiawah Island in South Carolina.

They were two distinctly different experiences. In the first, I was in the heat of battle, buoyed by all those chest-swelling feelings of national pride. In the second, I watched helplessly from the sidelines, pulling hard for my American pals, but feeling for my European friends as well. Both occasions were full of dramatic moments that created conversation for months afterward, and both left me with strong opinions about the true purpose of this international competition.

I remember how thrilled I was to make the team in 1985. While I hadn't won any tournaments that year, I had lost a playoff to Curtis Strange at the Honda Classic, and had several other top tens. But it was still touch-and-go for me, heading into the last qualifying tournament, the PGA at Cherry Hills. A tie for 10th there nailed down my spot on the team.

I was really anxious to get to Britain for the competition because my few trips over there had been so enjoyable. This was the year after I'd led the Open in the first round in 1984, and just two months after I'd finished eighth in the Open at Royal St. George's (and gone one-on-one with that streaker).

As much as anything, I liked playing in Britain because the fans were so friendly. They were always quick to applaud a good shot, and showed compassion when a player's luck went bad. The Brits were known for going out of their way to be cordial to American players competing in their most important event. This made what happened at the 1985 Ryder Cup matches at The Belfry all the more surprising: our American team received a less than gracious welcome.

For instance, when Curtis and I were introduced at the first tee of an alternate-shot match, we received only a smattering of applause. You'd have thought they introduced us not as America's Best Golfers, but as America's Most Wanted. Then our opponents, Paul Way and Ian Woosnam, were introduced, and they got a huge ovation. And so it went all weekend. The only times the crowd really cheered an American golfer was when he missed a putt or hit a ball into the water. I understood that national pride was at stake, but this was still just a golf match.

Perhaps the cumulative weight of recent history had finally caved in on the British, because in the thirteen matches before that year, the U.S. team had a record of twelve wins, no losses, and just one tie, even though the European team had been achingly close in the 1983 match, bowing by a 14½–13½ score on American soil. So 1985 was the year the Europeans were certain they could win the Cup, and the crowd was determined to do all it could to help.

I must say it bothered me to be treated that way, after I'd played so well the previous season to win a spot in the competition. It just went against everything I felt the Ryder Cup was supposed to represent, which was a sharing of abilities and a celebration of accomplishment among the top players from the two continents. I thought the matches would have an Olympic Games flavor, in which the competition was intense but the sportsmanship outstanding. The British and American press had stirred up the crowd with a nationalistic furor, however, and I think the gallery's aggressiveness caught even the European team off guard.

The notion that there was strong animosity between the Americans and Europeans had been given wide play in the British tabloids, but was just a figment of some writers' imaginations. I consider guys like Seve Ballesteros, Bernhard Langer, Nick Faldo, Sandy Lyle, and Sam Torrance to be friends, and in nearly every other circumstance in which we play against one another, the nationalism part of it has no relevance. Europe's captain, Tony Jacklin, and players such as Woosnam and Manuel Pinero even apologized to us for the behavior of the fans.

For whatever reason, on the last day our guys had a horrible time on the final nine, and particularly on the 18th hole. Our late collapse caused us to lose several matches, and the Europeans captured the Cup by a score of 16½ to 11½. I lost my own singles match to Sandy Lyle 3 and 2. While it was no fun losing, I didn't feel it was the end of the world, either. In fact, the European victory provided a good boost for international golf, because it pumped a tremendous amount of public interest back into an event that had been totally one-sided for decades.

When the American team lost again in 1987—for the first time ever on American soil—and had another final hole collapse in 1989, which led to a tie and the Europeans retaining the Cup, the media started stoking the fires of nationalism. Several articles appeared that really stuck it to the Americans, and every writer had his own opinion about why the Europeans had regained the upper hand.

I felt there were two basic reasons. The first one was obvious: in 1979, eligibility for the Great Britain–Ireland team was expanded to include all British PGA/European Tournament Players Division members who were residents of European nations. This not only greatly enriched the talent pool but brought in perhaps the fiercest Ryder Cup competitor ever in Ballesteros. His leadership, which inspired other newly eligible teammates such as Langer, Pinero, Jose Maria Canizares, and Jose Maria Olazabal, was analogous to adding Magic Johnson to a basketball team. Not only would Seve win, but he'd raise the level of the other players.

The second reason was more subtle, and dealt with golf course architecture and the type of course we're forced to play all too regularly on the U.S. tour. I'm referring, of course, to target golf courses, about which you've already heard me expound, where the design dictates the style of shot that has to be hit. If you're standing on a tee and you have water in front and back and water to the right and left, there's only one style of shot that will work: the one that goes straight up and down with backspin. The result of playing so many courses like this is that American professionals have, by and large, become very unimaginative golfers. When you play in high wind, you don't want to put the ball in the air. So what have you got on a target golf course when the wind blows? An unplayable course.

They say these target courses require so much skill, but

they actually require less. You don't have to be a great shotmaker, like a Trevino or a Ballesteros or a Watson. The only skill you need is a mental toughness not to let those crazy bounces off railroad ties and humps on the greens drive you nuts. I swear, some of the courses in America have imported so much wood they are in danger of burning down.

As a result, the European players, who by necessity have learned to play all manner of approach shots and pitch-and-run shots, and therefore take a more creative approach to the game in general, had inched ahead of the Americans.

Anyway, after two years of intense hype and analysis and talk of revenge, by the time we got to Kiawah Island in late September 1991, all the players were incredibly uptight and just ready to get on with it. It was really a nerve-wracking week. Little things got magnified, as every journalist from both continents was fighting to get a scoop.

At one point, Paul Azinger heard that Johnny Miller had criticized him during the opening day, and Paul said, under his breath, "Johnny Miller's the biggest moron on the air." A writer overheard it, and it made the papers. Paul, being the classy guy that he is, got up much earlier than normal and went looking for Johnny so he could apologize.

Meantime, Bob Trumpy walked in and picked up the newspaper and inserted a big M in the middle of "moron," and announced to everyone that it had been a misprint, that Azinger had actually called Miller "the biggest Mormon on the air." We all credited Trumpy with the best save of the week, better even than the par that Corey Pavin made on the 17th hole the last day to win his match and earn a crucial point for the U.S. Fortunately, all parties were able to put the incident behind them, but not until entire forests of trees had been sacrificed to provide enough paper to fully critique the episode.

We heard a lot of "Let's kill the Europeans," that week, and flags were being waved everywhere. There were also several allusions to Desert Storm, as though these matches remotely resembled the stakes of the Iraqi conflict. Most of the players felt that everything had been terribly over-blown.

The fact that the matches were played on a Pete Dye course that was very difficult under the best of conditions only added to the stress.

It was by far the toughest assignment I've had in broad-casting. I'm more used to events such as the Skins Game in Palm Springs, where the weather is perfect and the players are in a light mood. The journalistic challenge there usually doesn't reach beyond asking Nicklaus, after he's won five skins with a birdie putt, "Uh, Jack. How does it feel to win $170,000 and a Lady Rolex for Barbara?"

The Ryder Cup, on the other hand, was all business.

Anyway, the design of the course made it difficult on me and my fellow foot soldiers—Mark McCumber, Roger Maltbie, Mark Rolfing and Trumpy—who were tracking the various matches. On both nines, the routing went away from the clubhouse for five holes, then back to it the last four. We would lose power by getting so far from the truck, so we had to carry battery packs around our waist and trek over and through the sand dunes like Rommel through the desert. I was fighting the allergies that had infected my throat, and the sand and dirt did wonders for my voice. My periodic updates sounded like Joe Cocker with a head cold.

Having played in the Ryder Cup the one time, I can say I felt more nervous just watching these matches. That was because all of these guys were my friends, including the Europeans, and I could see how uptight everyone was. The media attention and public interest was greater than any major championship of which I had been a part.

The last day, naturally, everything was magnified even more. I walked along with the Ballesteros–Wayne Levi match, which had importance beyond its own point value. I said on the air that even though Wayne was not playing well, and was behind in the match at the turn, he could greatly help the American team merely by extending Ballesteros late into the round. As I said, Seve is a great cheerleader and a tremendous motivator to his teammates, and everyone knew that if he won early, he would go back out to the most critical match he could find and give the European player a big morale boost. If you've got Ballesteros standing by your bag looking at you with that gleam in his eye, saying, "C'mon, you can do it!" you're going to hit better shots.

Well, Wayne did just what he needed to. He made a couple of back nine birdies and he had about an eight-footer for par on the 14th hole to pull even. Although he missed the putt and eventually lost, 3 and 2, he still achieved something important by hanging in there like that.

Another outstanding incident was a confrontation between Seve and Ray Floyd on the 16th hole. Mark James was playing Lanny Wadkins; Seve had just finished, and Floyd had lost earlier in the day to Nick Faldo, and they were both on the scene. Mark James hit it over the green into a sandy area, where a lot of people had been tramping over the ground. His ball was sitting down, so he requested a ruling. During play, a competitor is allowed to receive direction only from his team captain, which for the Europeans was Bernard Gallacher, but Seve walked right over and started talking to Mark, trying to pump him up.

Having been the U.S. captain in 1989, Raymond was going to have none of this, so he stepped in there and hit him with the Evil Eye. Seve hesitated, then went back to talking to Mark again, so Ray turned up the heat about fifty degrees on his glare and took another step forward. Seve could now tell without reservation that Floyd was dead serious, so he sat down and got real quiet. Here were two of the most competitive guys in the history of golf standing jawbone to jawbone. I half-expected them to face away from each other, take six giant steps, turn, and at the count of three, fire!

However, nothing compared to the intensity of the Hale Irwin–Bernhard Langer match coming down the stretch. That was the most dramatic two holes of golf I've ever seen. They came to the 17th hole with Irwin one up, and the U.S. needing him to do no worse than tie his match to reclaim the Ryder Cup. On a nearly impossible hole which required a one-iron shot over water with about a thirty-mile-per-hour crosswind, Irwin missed the green left and Langer hit the fringe on the left side. Hale hit a good chip about eight feet away, but missed the putt, then Bernhard made an absolute must five-footer to stay alive. Those types of putts have less to do with technique than with the size of your heart.

Nearly everybody remembers the last hole. It was as though a Hollywood scriptwriter had penned those last fifteen minutes for the golf movie equivalent of *High Noon* or *Rocky*. It all came down to only lonely man, Bernhard Langer, standing over a six-footer with the fate of two continents in his hands. He makes the putt, and Europe earns a tie and retains the Cup, and the Americans have to listen to two more years of grief from a legion of armchair critics. He misses the putt, and the Americans are heroic and a monkey the size of King Kong is off their backs.

What can you say? Bernhard hit a good putt, and it missed. Never had it been more vividly dramatized that golf is a game of inches. Normally the Cup is determined while matches are still in progress, so what were the odds when the competition began that it would come down to the last group on the last day with the last player on the last hole hitting the last shot for all the marbles? That's pretty amazing, if you think about it.

To Bernhard's credit, he handled himself beautifully in the moments and days and weeks following the matches. In fact, he won the next tournament in which he played. The guy is a true champion, in every respect.

Anyway, when Langer was over his putt, I was kneeling on the side of the green next to Payne Stewart, Fred Couples, and Mark O'Meara. It was hard to watch. But when it missed and everybody erupted at once, it got downright scary. It was like one of those rock concerts with festival seating. I had the feeling if anybody fell down he'd be trampled to death. And yet I couldn't be concerned about any of that because I wasn't done working. I was hearing Larry Cirillo and Terry O'Neil from NBC yelling through my headphones to grab anybody on either team for an interview.

I managed to get to Mark and Sheryl Calcavecchia, and Mark was about the most relieved guy on the planet. He'd spent the previous hour in a state of despair, thinking he was going to be the goat if the Americans lost. Mark had lost the last four holes to end up tied with Colin Montgomerie, and it looked for a while that the half-point would cost the U.S. Fate had smiled on him, however, just as it had frowned on Bernhard a moment before. Amidst the pandemonium I congratulated Mark for his contributions to the victory, and he thanked me and finished his quart of Pepto-Bismol.

I've been asked a few times whether I was jealous I wasn't on the team. Obviously, I'd rather have been carrying a driver in my hand than a microphone, but I'm not sure I would have wanted to be in Hale Irwin's shoes playing the 18th hole with all that at stake. I'm a competitor, but I could barely breathe, and all I had to do was walk down the fairway.

It was intense. There's no other word for it.

CHAPTER 16

Off-Camera

TELEVISION HAS CAPTURED many of the great moments in golf over the last two decades, but often it's the subtle moments away from the footlights that are the most character-revealing.

When I started on the Tour at the beginning of 1977, Tom Watson had won just two official titles in the U.S. and one British Open. That season, however, he took off on an incredible eight-year run in which he won twenty-nine times, including two Masters, a U.S. Open, and four more British Opens. He was named Player of the Year six times in that stretch. It's no surprise that Tom quickly became my idol. He was realizing the dreams of every professional golfer, and doing it with style.

I jump at the chance to play practice rounds with Tom because I learn so much just by watching him. He's very aggressive with his swing. He once told me something that he'd learned from Byron Nelson: that it's always better when you're under the heat to hit less club and swing hard, than it is to take more club and swing soft. With the harder swing, you're more inclined to make a natural, athletic move at the ball.

When Tom was winning everything, I heard him say something at a clinic that went to the heart of his positive attitude. He said it never bothered him to miss a green because one of four things could happen, and three of them were good: he could hole the shot from off the green or out of the bunker, he could hit it close and tap in, he could hit it poorly and make a good putt, or he could hit it poorly and miss the putt. He said if you added up all those scores—a birdie, two pars, and a bogey—it came to even-par. So if you practiced your short game, you had nothing to fear. If I had to choose one player to hit a life-or-death five-foot putt, it would be Tom Watson in his prime. The guy had absolutely no fear.

Tom's always been a manly type of golfer, sort of like Palmer. He's strong, he hits the ball a mile, and he doesn't lag his putts. One day in a practice round at Colonial, we were walking down the second fairway and he said to his caddie Bruce Edwards, "Bruce, give me a Bandit." Bruce flipped him something, which he stuck in his mouth.

I asked him what it was, and he said, "It's a Skoal Bandit. Here, try one." Well, I figured if it was good enough for Watson, then it couldn't hurt Jacobsen. It was a little bag about the size of a Chiclet with tobacco in it, and I stuck it between my cheek and gum just as Tom had done. In about thirty seconds, my mouth was a burning truckload of jalapeñas, and I was spitting and coughing off to the side of the green. My head looked like Linda Blair's just before the priest jumped out the window.

Tom chuckled and looked at me like I was a sissy. The rest of the day, between gulps of water, I watched him with that Bandit in his mouth, and I never once saw him spit. He apparently swallowed all the juice. That was all the proof I needed that the guy had a cast-iron stomach.

I'm constantly impressed by the ability of Tom Kite to wring the most out of every round. I remember when Bob Gilder holed that shot for double-eagle at Westchester when Kite and I were chasing him. I thought, hey, that's kinda cool—a double-eagle. Then I looked over at Kite, and he had a perturbed look on his face. The only thing Gilder's miracle shot meant to him was that he'd just fallen at least two more strokes behind in his quest to win the tournament. His reaction caused me to question whether I had the right attitude.

Kite is one of the best golfers, pound for pound, that ever played the game. He's earned every single penny of his record winnings through hard work and discipline. Guys like Nicklaus and Palmer give the impression they fell out of their cribs with exceptional ability, an innate talent to win, and all the requisite charisma and class that goes with being a champion. It's second nature to them. But when you look at Tom, you don't think that. If Tom has a fifty-gallon drum of potential, he's using forty-eight gallons of it. Percentage-wise, no one else comes close.

I also want to say that Tom Kite is a tremendous individual. Despite the times he's been overlooked—such as the 1992 Masters and the 1991 Ryder Cup—when he finally won the Open at Pebble Beach he didn't change one bit. That's not always the case. Sometimes guys have personality transplants after they win a major, or they assume their IQ rises as they climb up the money list. The week after Pebble, Tom honored his commitment to play in the Buick Classic at Westchester, even though he probably would have preferred to go back to Texas and celebrate with his friends and family. As usual, he finished in the Top Ten.

Fuzzy Zoeller is one of the great characters in the game. How many men can say they won both the Masters and the U.S. Open, and gave the gallery some big laughs along the way? One of his classiest moves ever was at Winged Foot in 1984, when Greg Norman holed a putt on the last hole from off the green, with Zoeller watching from the fairway. Fuzzy thought Greg had made birdie, which would likely have won Norman the tournament, so he held a white towel above his head and waved it in surrender. The crowd roared in delight. Actually, Greg had saved par, and they ended up in an eighteen-hole playoff the next day, which Fuzzy won easily by shooting 67. The point is that Fuzzy didn't hang his head when Greg's putt went in; he showed the class of a true sportsman with a great sense of humor.

Fuzzy may be the best needler on the Tour. In the Merrill Lynch Shoot-Outs, he's incorrigible. If he decides to use you as bait for his jokes, you just pray you're eliminated on the first hole, because the abuse you take is not worth the prize money.

Fuzzy tore into Craig Stadler once during our pre-round clinic at the Fred Meyer Challenge. We'd been playing in a lot of rain in the previous weeks, and Craig had been on the road for about two months with the same pair of shoes. Those babies had been through several rain delays and traipsing through mud puddles and they looked more brown than white, with lots of cracks in them. Fuzzy yelled out, "Nice clods, Stadler. Did you get those at a Buster Brown fire sale?"

The Walrus didn't miss a beat. He immediately kicked off his shoes and threw them at Fuzzy and began hitting balls in his stocking feet. Fuzzy picked one of the shoes up, crinkled his nose, and lobbed it and its mate back over his head into the grandstands. I'm certain that to this day those shoes are being worn by some avid golfer at Gopher Creek Muny, who tells his buddies they once belonged to Craig Stadler and were a personal gift to him from Fuzzy Zoeller.

I also remember a time in 1981, just after Bobby Knight's Indiana Hoosiers had beaten Dean Smith's North Carolina Tar Heels in the NCAA basketball finals, that Fuzzy, who's from New Albany, Indiana, showed up at the Greensboro N.C. pro-am wearing a T-shirt that said, "Bobby Knight 1, Dean Smith 0." It was the equivalent of wearing a Black Power shirt to a Ku Klux Klan rally. Somehow, though, with that big grin on his face, Fuz pulled it off without creating a riot.

I can't think of Fuzzy's gesture in the Open without recalling Hale Irwin's monster putt at Medinah in the 1990 U.S. Open and his unbridled hand-slapping lap around the 18th green. Hale didn't know whether the putt meant he'd won or not; he just knew his regulation 72 holes had ended on a big high and that he might have made the biggest putt of his life. The thing I liked about the celebration was that it was purely spontaneous, and it gave so much back to those fans that were there.

Like Raymond Floyd, Hale's a big inspiration to those of us in our late thirties. He's proof that older can mean better if you keep plugging away.

*   *   *

What stands out about Ben Crenshaw, for me, is his intense love for the history and traditions of the game. A lot of times on the Mondays and Tuesdays before tournaments, when many guys are playing in pro-ams or Shoot-Outs or just working on their yardages or getting the feel of the greens, Ben will go to other golf courses in the area simply because he hasn't played them before. He'll call ahead and set up a game with the host pro or the club champion or just a couple members of the club. He likes to look at all the distinctive design features and learn about the history of the course. Much of what he picks up he incorporates in the courses he designs, such as the spectacular Plantation course at Kapalua.

Because he has such respect for the traditions of golf, I would say Ben's Masters win in 1984 meant more to him than any major has to a player before. Ben had been close in majors so many times, and to win a tournament with that much history was really special.

Of all Mark O'Meara's victories, the one that stands out for me is the 1990 AT&T Pebble Beach National Pro-Am. His father Bob played with him as his partner, and they made the cut. You could sense how proud Bob was walking down the 18th hole the last day with his son in command.

I'll especially remember Mark, and his wife Alicia, for being so nice to my dad when we went to Japan for the U.S. vs. Japan team competition in 1984. They sort of adopted him and did whatever they could to make him comfortable, as did his parents, Bob and Nelda. Dad had had his first cancer surgery and had to be fed with a liquid poured through a tube in his stomach, but even with all his infirmities, he was a great cheerleader and a wonderful inspiration to the American team, so much so that my teammates named him our honorary captain. When we all toasted sake to celebrate the victory, Dad ignored his doctor's orders and had us pour some through the tube in his stomach. Then he shrugged and said, "Heck with it," and put a cup to his lips. I had to carry him off the team bus and tuck him in bed when we got back to the hotel, but he had a big smile on his face as he fell asleep.

I've told many Lee Trevino stories already, but there's one moment with him I'll never forget. I was having my best tournament ever in 1978 at the B.C. Open, and was in solid contention after two rounds. I found myself paired with Trevino on Saturday—the first time I'd played with him. Going down the ninth fairway, I was three under for the day and Lee was three over. Rather than cop an attitude, though, he said to me, "How long you been out here?" I told him it was my second year. He said, "You've got a good swing. I think you're going to have a good career out here."

That was shocking enough, but then he said, "Look, this isn't my day, but I've had plenty of good ones in the past and I'll have plenty more in the future. Why don't you just win this darned thing?"

I didn't win—Kite did—but I finished third and earned my biggest check ever on the Tour. Even greater than the high finish was the thrill I got from Trevino's generous comment. Since I've gotten to know Lee as a friend through the years, I see how typical that gesture was. Although he guards his privacy, he tries to be nice to everyone. Lee's family comes first with him, but everybody else, whether it's a corporate CEO or the locker room attendant, is tied for second.

*   *   *

I'd be remiss if I didn't recount an incredible stretch of
holes Johnny Miller had with me in the Chrysler Team
Championship in 1989. After a poor first 36 holes, we had
an equally poor start on Saturday and had no chance of
making the 54-hole cut. That is, until Johnny experienced
déjà vu from the mid-1970s. He birdied five straight, from
the ninth to the thirteenth, we parred fourteen, and I
birdied fifteen. I then hit a long-iron one foot from the
hole at the 220-yard sixteenth. Knowing I had the birdie
locked up, Johnny pulled out a one-iron and merely
knocked it in the cup for an ace. After a quick celebration,
he finished with birdies on the 17th and 18th holes. We
had played the last ten holes in ten under par, and Miller
had played them in nine-under, to make the cut right on
the number.

Don't think for a minute Johnny's all through as a
player, just because he's wearing a headset on weekends. If
his chronically bad legs hold up, he'll grab his share of
victories on the Senior Tour in a few years.

It's fantastic that Gene Sarazen, this rare man who competed head-to-head with the likes of Walter Hagen and
Bobby Jones and won all four major professional championships, is still active at ninety. I see Mr. Sarazen at least
once a year, at the Masters.

Last year at Augusta, I was in the first twosome to play
on Thursday, paired with Dillard Pruitt. When we walked
onto the first tee, he was seated chatting with Byron Nelson and Ken Venturi. Sarazen had hit the ceremonial drive
off the first tee, and they were sort of holding court. Now,
I proudly represent Toyota on the Tour, and as always I

was wearing a Toyota visor. I shook hands with all of the legends, then Mr. Sarazen said (mainly for the benefit of the others), "How much do they pay you to wear that visor, a million bucks?"

His comment kind of took me back, but I just said, "I wish it *was* a million, Mr. Sarazen."

Then he turned around and jokingly said, "Aw, you young kids will put anything on your heads for the right price."

This, of course, got a wry laugh from the others, because when you're ninety years old and as well liked as Gene Sarazen, nearly anything you say is funny.

Although I was thinking that Toyotas didn't exist in his day or he certainly would have accepted their endorsement money, I walked over to my bag, took off my visor, and handed it to Mike. "Mr. Sarazen," I said, "out of respect for you I will play this first hole without my visor."

He just chuckled, but Venturi winked at me, as though I'd done the right thing. I mean what else could I have done? We're talking about a man who had won the U.S. Open seventy years before, in 1922. I'd say that deserves respect.

If ever there was an original on the Tour, it's Chi Chi Rodriguez. Every time I see him, he's surrounded by several kids he's taken under his wing, but it's certainly not just for show. He owns and staffs a youth foundation in Florida, and he constantly imparts wisdom to those children so they can lead constructive lives. He is truly a pied piper.

Last year at the Fred Meyer Challenge clinic, Chi Chi cracked everyone up when Larry Mize was demonstrating how to chip. "Greg Norman has to turn his head when Larry's chipping," he said, alluding to Mize's miracle shot which robbed Greg of the 1987 Masters. "Greg's the Great White Shark, but I'm the Loan Shark."

I was playing with Chi Chi once when he ripped a five-iron dead at the flag, but the ball landed on the back of the green and bounced over. As he calmly handed his club to his caddy, he said, "Right string, wrong yo-yo."

He also likes to have fun with his impoverished upbringing in Puerto Rico. He says, "Playing golf is not hot work. Cutting sugar cane for a dollar a day—that's hot work. Hotter than my first wristwatch." And, "Everyone knows Arnie Palmer loves Pennzoil. I think he drinks the stuff. And everyone knows he's got that old tractor . . . but I've got the hubcaps."

Isao Aoki may have the best short game in the world, due to a magical touch in his hands and wrists and the fact that he knows how to practice. He's given me bunker lessons through the years which have been very helpful, and he's generously shared time with dozens of other players who aspire to his wizardry around the greens.

One of Aoki's practice techniques in sand traps is to give himself horrible lies. He'll plug the ball or put it in a footprint or on a difficult downhill lie. There's no sand shot he could confront that would be totally unfamiliar.

I'll never forget the 1983 Hawaiian Open, when I played the final round with Jack Renner, in the second to last group. When Jack finished at 19 under par, it looked like he had the tournament won. We were in the scorer's tent signing our cards as Aoki was playing the par-five 18th hole and needing a birdie to tie. But he was lying two in the rough, some 130 yards from the green. I congratulated Renner, thinking he had probably won the golf tournament or, at worse, was looking at sudden death.

Just then a huge scream went up, and Tom Seaver, who was on NBC's broadcast team, said to me, "It's in!" And Renner turned to me and said, *"Where* is it?" And with a feeling of sympathy, I replied, "It's in." And Jack said, "It's in *what?"* He quickly realized, as the crowd continued to go bananas, exactly where Aoki's shot had gone—right into the hole and right through his heart. Aoki's miracle enabled him to be the first player from Japan ever to win on the PGA Tour.

To Renner's credit, he behaved with great composure, despite the shocking setback. In fact, he returned to Hawaii the next year and won the tournament.

When I first started playing in Europe, Nick Faldo was having a horrible time with the British press and tabloids. The scrutiny on him was intense because he and Sandy Lyle represented Britain's hope for the future. Although Nick had won his share of tournaments, he had also lost some, and the press dubbed him Nick "Foldo." I remember reading these cruel stories and seeing the agony on his face as he withstood the unfair criticism.

Faldo has clearly had the last laugh in every respect, because since 1987 he has won five major championships, and exhibited a sharp sense of humor as well. When Nick won the 1992 British Open with a strong finish, after losing a sizeable final-round lead, he said that had he lost, "I might have become a fishing pro. There's no pressure dragging out trout."

Then he added, alluding to his past treatment, "I'd like to thank the media from the heart of my bottom."

While it's easy to joke after a victory, Nick is also capable of humor in adversity. In the U.S. Open at Pebble Beach, he climbed a tree to try to identify his golf ball on the 14th hole of the second round. Balanced precariously on a limb, he looked around and said, "Where the hell is Jane?" He ended up with a triple-bogey eight, which seriously hurt his chances of winning the tournament, but he could still appreciate the humor of his predicament.

Faldo does things his own way. His caddy, Fannie Sunesson, is the only full-time female caddy among the top players, and Nick and his instructor, David Leadbetter, have elevated the standards of teacher-pupil relationships. Through their joint commitment to excellence, both have reached their common goal—to be the best in the world in their given professions.

There are dozens of Raymond Floyd stories I could tell about heroic moments on the golf course, but most fans already know them. I like one that had nothing to do with golf. Several years ago, we were flying back from the British Open, and I was seated in the row in front of Ray, his wife Maria, and his daughter Christina, who was eight at the time. Christina was intently doing the hair on one of her dolls. I told her that she was quite the hairstylist. She thanked me and asked if she could do mine.

We had a long flight ahead of us, so I thought, why not. Christina moved up and sat next to me and for the next forty-five minutes she put ribbons and barrettes in my hair and gave me the full salon treatment. I stopped her just before she went for the lipstick and eye-liner. I then peered over the seat at Ray to get his opinion of my new coiffure. He just gave me that famous laser stare of his, but he couldn't hold it. After a few seconds, his face broke into a big grin, and he said, "Peter, you're nuts."

I wish I could have seen Tommy Bolt play in his prime. He was one of the purest ball-strikers ever. I have played with him a few times, however, and watched him hit a lot of balls when I was on the NBC broadcast team at the Legends of Golf in Austin, Texas. There are so many hilarious stories about "Lightning" Bolt's temper that every time he's around, his contemporaries relive a few. I heard this one in the locker room at the Legends:

It seems that back in the 1950s some of the women score keepers who follow along with the players had complained to Tour officials about Tommy passing gas on the golf course . . . loudly. So one of the officials came to Tommy and gave him a warning. He said, "Tommy, if we hear any more complaints, we're going to have to fine you." Tommy just laughed about it. It wasn't like fines were a novelty to Bolt. He included them in his annual budget. Anyway, at the next tournament, sure enough, Tommy's breakfast was not agreeing with him once again, and a woman scorer filed a complaint after the round. Soon thereafter, an official approached Bolt.

"Tommy, we're gonna have to fine you $100," he said.

"What on earth for?" Tommy said. "Simply for doing something natural?"

The official said, "Well, it wasn't so much the farting that upset the lady. It was the fact that you kept lifting your leg and clutching your thigh in celebration."

As Bolt handed over a C-note, he turned to the other two golfers in his threesome, who were falling off their chairs laughing, and said, "Damn, they're trying to take all the color out of the game."

*   *   *

One year when I was playing in the Johnnie Walker Cup in Madrid, Gary Player and his wife Vivienne invited Jan and me to dinner. We were in a restaurant and Gary was preaching, as he often does, about the benefits of exercise and a proper diet. Suddenly, Vivienne interrupted and said, "C'mon, Gary. Don't bore Peter with these stories."

Then she turned to me and said, "He's not as fanatical as he says. Every time Gary returns to South Africa from the States, he brings an extra bag to carry all the Snickers, Three Musketeers, Kit-Kats, and Reese's Peanut Butter Cups he can smuggle in."

Gary was squirming and trying to get her to stop, but she was on a roll.

"And you know he has a special chocolate cabinet in the house with a lock on it, and whenever he leaves he takes the key," she said. "So one day I picked the lock and took a couple of candy bars. Five minutes after he'd returned, he came to me and said, 'Vivienne, someone's broken into my cabinet and stolen two Snickers bars. I know, because there were thirty-nine when I left and there's only thirty-seven now.' "

Jan and I were cracking up, and by this time so was Gary. "A little sweet tooth won't kill a man," he said, "as long as you do one hundred pushups and eat your granola in the morning."

When Seve Ballesteros is on, he's the most creative player in the game. I've always enjoyed playing with him, and he's even given me a few short-game pointers through the years. Once, in Spain, it backfired on him. In 1981 (the same week Vivienne Player had exposed her husband's one vice), I won the Johnny Walker Cup. The next year I returned to defend in Barcelona. Seve is far more at ease on his home turf than he is in America. Early in the week he spent an hour and a half with me around a practice green, showing me different chip shots and bunker shots. He gave me pointers on ball position and technique that I still use today. As luck would have it, I was two shots behind him after 54 holes, and caught him the last day to win by one. The pointers he gave me clearly made the difference in the victory, but that shows the level of camaraderie that often exists between players.

Ian Woosnam is a throwback to some of his Irish and Welsh predecessors, who were proud to admit they enjoyed the 19th hole and the camaraderie that accompanies it. In other words, Ian's not averse to taking a sip from time to time with his golfing friends.

There's a story about Woosie being hired by the Sultan of Brunei, reputedly the world's wealthiest man, to give golf lessons to his nephew. The compensation for this instruction would be enough to launch a space program in a small country, but it was just ball-marker change to the Sultan. After all, a golfer ranked number one in the world, as Woosnam was at the time, doesn't come cheap. Anyway, knowing his client might balk at the offer if he knew all the pertinent facts, Ian's agent chose not to inform him that the country of Brunei is much like the state of Utah: drier than a camel's mouth.

Ian wasn't told of this deprivation until he had gotten on the plane to Brunei. Apparently, he avoided any unnecessary temperance by stocking up on the flight, and prevailing upon the "stewardi" to give him all the extra miniature bottles they could collect. By all accounts, Ian had a great time. There's been no word, however, on whether the Sultan's nephew cured his duck-hook.

The great Scottish player, Sandy Lyle, is one of my favorite people in golf, a man of honesty and integrity. In 1989, for instance, he didn't feel he deserved a spot on the European Ryder Cup team, so he asked not to be considered for one of the captain's selections. That showed real character.

Sometimes Sandy's honesty is very literal. Ask him a question, you get a straight answer.

A few years ago, Tony Jacklin, who had been Sandy's Ryder Cup captain, ran across Lyle in Kennedy Airport. They had not seen each other in months, and Tony was surprised to see his friend in New York. As they passed each other going in opposite directions, Jacklin waved to him and said, "Hey, Sandy, where are you going?"

Sandy replied, "To the toilet."

On another occasion, in 1987, a Jacksonville, Florida, radio personality was interviewing Sandy after winning the Players Championship. Sandy had also won the British Open in 1985. Some people consider The Players to be a fifth major championship, and that was where the interviewer was leading when he asked Lyle, "What's the difference between the British Open and the Players Championship?"

Sandy replied, "About 120 years."

The first time I saw John Cook play was in 1976, when I was caddying for my future brother-in-law, Mike Davis, in the Crosby. I remember this eighteen-year-old kid with long blond surfer hair playing with the pros, and how he was driving it past them and hitting it every bit as good as they were. He looked like a world-beater even then.

John is yet another example of a player who has learned from adversity and then taken his game to a higher level. After being sidelined most of 1989 by wrist surgery, Cook has played marvelous golf ever since, culminating in his great 1992 season, when he won three times and finished second at the British Open and PGA. John certainly didn't engage in self-pity when he was injured; in fact, he told me it was his most enjoyable year as a professional. He really liked seeing his kids go from day to day and week to week in their daily routines. It was much more rewarding for him than trying to play catch-up on their lives during weeks off his regular Tour schedule, as though he were watching a home video on fast-forward. How well I know. Like the Cooks, we have two girls and a boy, and when I'm gone for three weeks at a time, I feel like I've missed a chunk of life that I can never get back.

Because John has his priorities so well in place, I know he really appreciates his current success.

No American professional has played consistently better than Paul Azinger in the last six years. He's averaged well over $800,000 per season in that time, won eight tournaments, and shown he's bulletproof under pressure, first by beating Seve Ballesteros, and then Jose Maria Olazabal, in Ryder Cup singles matches in 1989 and 1991. But "Zinger" paid his dues to get to his present position. He and his wife Toni traveled the Tour in a motor home for four years in the early 1980s, and were subject to some humiliating incidents.

In 1982, at the Walt Disney World Golf Classic in

Florida, Paul had camped their "home" in the golf course parking lot early in the week. Sure enough, at two in the morning, six hours before an eight A.M. tee time, he got a knock on the door and a Disney World security guard soberly informed him that he'd have to move immediately. Paul explained that he was playing in the golf tournament, but got no sympathy from the guard and was forced to relocate to a church parking lot.

"I was so angry, I went about one mile an hour on my way out," Paul told me, "and that security guard was right on my bumper all the way to the front gate, making sure I didn't flip a U-turn and go back."

Another time, just after Paul had missed a 36-hole cut, he was napping in the back of the motor home as Toni was driving it out of town. She miscalculated and got the vehicle wedged in a toll booth. "The bang was so loud when we hit the overhang that our Persian cat Cleo jumped about two feet in the air and screeched in my face," Paul said. "When we backed out, the whole awning tore off . . . And they talk about the glamour of The Tour."

Azinger cites an off-course incident near the end of the 1986 season as turning his career around. Another player made a disparaging remark in the locker room, with several other players within earshot, suggesting that Paul had intentionally skipped the last tournament of the year so that he could retain a small lead in the Sand Saves statistical category, and thereby win a cash bonus. In reality, Paul had withdrawn from the tournament because his father had suffered a heart attack. Azinger told me his feelings were deeply hurt by the jab, and he determined that he would go about his business the next season with a killer instinct, looking out for only himself. The result was that he won three times, finished second in the British Open, and was named PGA Player of the Year in 1987.

Smiling, Paul said, "I wish I could find someone to tick me off like that again."

Every year at the Colonial there's a dinner honoring all past champions. Each Colonial winner receives a red plaid jacket, which I believe glows in the dark. I'm certain all the 1956 Buicks in Fort Worth are missing their upholstery because it went to make up those sportscoats. Before I won there in 1984, I remember kidding Fuzzy Zoeller on his way to the dinner. "Hey, Fuz, where'd you get the coat? Did you shoot a couch?"

But after I won a coat of my own, it suddenly became the best-looking garment I owned, and each year at the banquet I wear it with pride.

Anyway, Ben Hogan and his wife Valerie always sit on the top dais at the dinner, sometimes next to the defending champion. Although I'd seen Mr. Hogan several times, it wasn't until I was the defender that I got up the courage to introduce myself to him. I'm not one to ask for autographs, but I had him sign a visor for me when all the winners at Colonial posed with him a few years ago at the Wall of Champions. I wore that visor for the entire week of the tournament.

Professional golfers pride themselves on being able to work the ball left or right, hit it high or low, and generally hit whatever shot is required by the circumstance. However, Hogan had standards that were a clear level above everyone else's when it came to ball-striking. From talking to other players, and watching films of him, I believe he came the closest of anyone to hitting perfect golf shots on a consistent basis.

*   *   *

A trait of most of the great players is that they have to go through fire to get to the promised land. That certainly was the case with Payne Stewart. Before 1989, the caddies called him Avis because he finished second so often. I know that nickname really hurt him. I remember watching him double-bogey the final hole and lose a playoff to Bob Eastwood at the Byron Nelson in 1985, and how down he and his wife, Tracy, were afterwards. He also lost four other playoffs, including two at Colonial, before he won one. Despite those disappointments, though, he always handled himself with a lot of style.

The obvious breakthrough for him was at the PGA at Kemper Lakes in 1989. Although some people say Mike Reid gave away that tournament, don't forget that Payne shot 30 on the final nine and birdied the last hole. It was his great charge that put the heat on Reid.

I had finished earlier that day, and Jan and I were packing to leave our hotel as we watched the finish of the tournament. When Payne won, we decided to cancel the flight and return to the course to celebrate with him and Tracy. When he saw me, he greeted me with a big bear hug and his adrenaline was running so high I thought he'd broken about six of my ribs. We had a few glasses of champagne with them, and Payne's emotions were going up and down the scale. One minute he was high as a kite, and the next sentimental. He was thinking of his father, whom he'd lost to cancer a few years before. I could feel nothing but joy for my friend, who had at last made it through the fire to the promised land.

I got my first look at Curtis Strange when he won the 1974 NCAA title in San Diego as a freshman. He came to the last hole, a par-five, and was one behind Florida's Phil Hancock individually. He was told that a par would be good enough to win the team title. All Curtis did was hit a one-iron about eight feet from the hole and make the putt for eagle—to lock up both the team and individual titles.

When he failed to repeat as NCAA champion the following year, a writer said to him, "You can't win them all." Curtis stared a hole through him and said, "Why not?"

The next year I went to Japan with him as part of an American college all-star team, and on a cold, windy day when everyone was shooting 74s and 75s, Curtis went at it with Masahiro Kuramoto, who, incidentally, was co-medalist at the 1992 PGA Tour qualifier. The guy is about five-three with massive forearms, and he was by far the best college player the Japanese had to offer. They just kept firing away at each other and both ended up shooting 64. Neither one budged an inch. Curtis, it goes without saying, has industrial-strength testicles.

Curtis and Sarah traveled a lot with Jan and me when we were both starting out, and neither of us had any money. In Milwaukee we got fifteen-dollar-per-night rooms at the Edge-O-Town Motel—that was the actual name of it. To save money on food, we carried a portable hibachi on our travels, and one night had a cook-out on the corner down by the Pepsi machine. People kept walking by in bathrobes to fill up their buckets at the ice machine. That Friday, after we'd both made the cut, we celebrated in style—by dining out at the local pizza parlor.

What a contrast to a couple of years later, when Curtis and I went with then-touring pro Ron Cerrudo to a tournament hosted by the King of Morocco. It was quite a culture shock. For instance, we got in trouble for paying our teenage caddies a couple hundred bucks apiece; we had been instructed to pay them only three dollars a day, but we had felt that wasn't enough. It turned out it was so as not to create disharmony in their families—we had given them more money than their fathers made in an entire month!

We both finished in the top ten at that tournament, which meant we would be honored at the awards ceremony. Lee Trevino won, and was presented with an incredible jeweled saber from the King. It was inlaid with diamonds, rubies, and emeralds and must have been worth $50,000.

Curtis and I were drinking Moroccan beer, which will put hair on your teeth, and as the ceremony crept along, we couldn't hold it any longer and snuck out to the john. Our timing when we returned was not good. We walked back in just as the Prince and his entourage were making their grand entrance, and these rough-looking security guards grabbed us and demanded to know who we were and what we were doing. The movie *Midnight Express* had just been released, and it flashed in my mind that they were going to throw us into some Moroccan prison and violate us horribly and bite off our tongues. I remember thinking, why, oh why, did we have to finish in the top ten? Fortunately, everything was cleared up, and we were allowed back in. But we didn't drink any more Moroccan beer that night, I can tell you.

I love to kid Curtis about having uttered a few choice words on camera through the years. In the 1989 PGA, he called an intrusive photographer a son of a bitch, with a live mike about ten feet away. Two weeks later, we were at the Fred Meyer Challenge, when I called Curtis up at the clinic to hit a few. As he began to speak, I grabbed the microphone from him and said I couldn't trust him with it, what with all the women and children in attendance.

He took it good-naturedly, of course. Why, you can barely see the cleat-marks on my back anymore.

CHAPTER 17

A Candle in the Wind

THERE'S A LOT OF LEVITY and joy that goes with being a professional golfer, not to mention the many privileges afforded those who achieve success at the top levels of the sport. I've tried to bring to life in this book the flavor of several of these funny and triumphant moments.

But it would be misrepresenting the whole experience of the PGA Tour to imply that the men who compete out here are somehow exempt from the pain and sorrow of everyday living. Like all the players, I'm reminded from time to time that what we do every day—often with the solemn demeanor of heart surgeons—is nothing more than a game, and that the genuine business of life takes place outside the ropes, far removed from all the lights and cameras. This chapter is about the real world.

A lot of people know my older brother David. He played a year ahead of me on the University of Oregon golf team, and is still an excellent player in the Pacific Northwest.

David has competed in the U.S. Amateur, was a semifinalist in the U.S. Mid-Amateur a few years ago, and when I'm home and we play practice rounds together, I have to play my best or David will beat me out of my last month's Tour winnings.

My sister, Susie, is also a fine athlete, with a large circle of friends. Susie earned eleven varsity letters in high school and was all-state in lacrosse at Pitzer College in California. She twice played in the U.S. Junior and U.S. Women's Amateur golf championships and reached the semifinals of the Oregon women's amateur when she was just fifteen. She had the potential to play professional golf.

Much less is known about my younger brother, Paul, and there are reasons for that. Paul elected to live his life in relative quiet, apart from all the fuss and bother that I've come to accept as routine. I've never spoken publicly about Paul because I felt his story had to be told at the proper time and in the proper context. This book is the right place to tell Paul's story.

In one sense, it has nothing to do with my life as a golfer; in another, it has everything.

Peter and Paul: the two names are linked together all the way back to the Bible, and when brothers just two years apart are given those names, comparisons are inevitable. As much as every parent aspires to equal treatment of all their children in a good-sized family, it's impossible to ensure that each child gets his full share of attention. In Paul's case, I think it was difficult, because he had two very active older brothers to follow and to be compared against. David and I were both athletic, and involved in golf and other sports. We were both sports editors of the high school paper and took part in a number of other school activities. We made friends easily and had a relatively carefree time of it.

Paul, on the other hand, didn't care much for sports, and

was more introverted by nature. He had to listen to friends and teachers constantly asking, "Why aren't you like your older brothers?"

As the third boy in the Jacobsen family a lot was expected of Paul, and he just couldn't or didn't want to live up to it. So he went his own way, and, as too often happens these days, he eventually fell into problems with drugs.

As we got older, Paul and I drifted apart. We still loved each other, and stayed in contact, and I would hear from his friends that he was proud of what I had done in my career, but it was difficult for him to express that pride directly to me. It was very important to Paul that he establish his own identity. He didn't want to stay in Portland and have to be pestered with questions about being Peter's brother, and why Peter missed that five-footer on television last week, and all the other burdens that David and Susie put up with all the time.

So he moved to Los Angeles and got a job as a graphic artist, and did some modeling on the side. In Southern California he could be just Paul Jacobsen, and have his own life. I thought it was a courageous thing to do, and I admired him for it.

However, there was a certain tension between Paul and the rest of the family that wouldn't go away. When Jan and I would go to Los Angeles each year for the L.A. Open, it seemed that Paul was usually too busy to come out to the course to watch me play. It was his way of telling me that his life was much more important than coming to a golf tournament, and I understood. We would always talk on the phone when we were in town, but that was about it.

About ten years ago, when Paul was twenty-six, he just blurted something out in a phone conversation with me. "You know I'm gay, don't you?" he said.

And I told him that, of course, I knew, and that it was

no big deal to me. Although I was surprised that he had told me so suddenly, I was glad for him that he could get it off his chest. It meant he was coming to grips with his life and facing who he was.

Paul's problems with drugs and alcohol grew worse through the years, and it was not uncommon for us to get phone calls from him at three or four in the morning. These would start out normally enough, with "Hi, how're ya doin'," then quickly deteriorate into bouts of ranting at us about all the problems in his life. He would get irrational and start calling us names. Mom and Dad would get the calls, or David or Susie, or whomever he could reach on the phone. He was using a lot of cocaine during the day, and drinking vodka at night to come down from it, and just hurling himself around on this emotional rollercoaster.

It got so bad in late 1987 that we checked him into the Betty Ford Clinic in Palm Springs. Thankfully, through the good work of the people there, Paul got clean. He seemed to be getting his life back on track in 1988, when I got the phone call that changed everything.

It was August 24, the day after the Fred Meyer Challenge. Mom called to say that Paul had been admitted to the hospital with pneumonia. Jan and I were immediately concerned that he might have AIDS. I called Paul and he sounded upbeat and said he thought he'd been living on too fast a track and needed to slow down and rest. He even talked about moving back to the Northwest. However, by the next week, when I was in Toronto for the Canadian Open, the news was all bad. Paul did, in fact, have AIDS and had been admitted to the intensive care unit at Cedars Sinai Hospital. I was worthless in Canada, and withdrew after shooting a first-round 79. My mind had never been further from a golf course than it was that day.

I flew back to Portland, and Jan and I caught the first flight to Los Angeles to be with Paul.

I had heard from friends that Paul's weight was down, and that he had not been in good health for a while, but seeing him in the hospital was a shock. I hadn't seen him since we'd checked him into the Betty Ford Center eight months before, and it was obvious that his condition was critical. He had lost a lot of weight and was extremely gaunt. In hindsight, I think Paul had known he was seriously ill for months before he was tested, but his fear of learning the truth was so great that he put off going to the doctor. By the time he was examined, he had full-blown AIDS.

Despite his drug problems, Paul had always stayed in shape with regular exercise, but now he was so thin and pale. He had lost more than thirty pounds off a slight frame. It broke my heart to see him. I told Jan that we better put all our plans on hold, because we really needed to be with Paul.

An especially vivid memory is of walking into his room and seeing him hooked up to a respirator. He looked up at me with terror in his eyes. Then he wrote something on a pad and handed it to me. It said, "Peter, you can do anything. Please make this go away."

My eyes filled with tears, then Paul put his arms around me and hugged me real tight. It was the most powerless feeling I'd ever had. Here, my kid brother was telling me I could do anything, but there wasn't a damn thing I could do to help him when he most needed it. I couldn't find anything to say, and I started to cry. I finally choked out something like, "Paul, we'll do everything we can for you."

The poor guy was just so scared and desperate. I'll never forget that look in his eyes.

I stayed in his room for several hours at a time, and we all took turns being with him. Then we'd return to the hotel, catch a nap, and go back. Just the third day after we'd arrived, Paul took a horrible turn for the worse. He'd been fighting the respirator, which, of course, he needed to keep breathing, and the doctors had just started using a paralyzing drug on him so that his body would relax and he'd be better able to fight the pneumonia. Then he suddenly slipped into a coma.

We went home that evening, aware that the end was near. It was September 5, just twelve days after I'd been told of Paul's illness and only a week since he'd been diagnosed. I was sound asleep when something unusual happened. At exactly one-thirty in the morning, I woke up suddenly and felt a fluttering movement inside my body. I asked Jan to turn on the light, and I told her that Paul was with us.

I said, "He's inside of me."

"Are you all right?" she asked.

I was oddly at peace. I told her that Paul had come there to tell me everything was okay, and that he was fine. I also told her I just wanted to lie there for a moment and feel the spirit of my brother, because that's exactly what it was. Paul's spirit was with me, and it was comforting.

I remember the fluttering movement didn't go away, it was almost like butterflies inside of me, and then I faded off to sleep. When I awoke the next morning, Jan asked if I remembered waking up the previous night, and I recalled it all perfectly. I told her Paul had come to visit me, and that he was finally out of his pain, but that he had left something with me.

That morning I called one of Paul's close friends, who lives on a farm in the state of Washington, and before she heard my experience she told me that she had been awakened the previous night by an owl that had flown down and landed on her open windowsill and started to hoot into the room. An owl is universally regarded as a sign of death. I asked her what time it had happened, and she said one-thirty.

Later in the day, I talked to Paul's roommate, and he said that the dog and cat had been going crazy all week without Paul there, and that the animals had been keeping him awake at night. But at one-thirty in the morning, they had suddenly calmed down. He said he felt Paul's spirit had been with them.

It's extraordinary that three different people who were close to my brother—one of them a thousand miles away—felt his presence at the same time.

When we went to the hospital, one of Paul's nurses told me that his vital signs had dropped sharply at one-thirty in the morning. "In my opinion, he has left us," she said.

Paul never came out of his coma, and died peacefully later that day. He was thirty-two years old.

The sorrow of his death was eased for me by the certain knowledge that he'd visited me. Paul had said something to me that night that I remember distinctly. "Peter, you're okay just the way you are," he said. "Be nice to people and don't let anything get you down." And then he said, "Go out there and win. Just go out there and win."

The official cause of Paul's death listed on the certificate was pneumonia, so it was never revealed in the Portland newspaper that he had died of AIDS. That was because Paul told me he didn't want my children or David's children, all of whom were very young, to have to deal with the stigma of his disease. Paul knew that kids can be cruel about things like that, and he was sensitive enough to want the cause of his death concealed until David and I felt the children were ready to hear about it. We told my oldest daughter Amy, who is now twelve, but we waited to tell the others until this book was published.

Naturally, we told the true circumstances of Paul's illness to his close friends and our relatives immediately after he died.

We had a small burial service for him in Hollywood, as he'd requested, and a larger service at Trinity Church in Portland. All the family members spoke, even my dad. Although Paul and Dad had had a rocky relationship, it was important to my father to make some final comments about his youngest son.

There was my dad in his fourth year of fighting cancer, with half his tongue removed, speaking to all assembled about the death of his youngest son, and how he loved him. Dad's speech was hard to understand, but the message wasn't in his words anyway. It was in the courage he showed just being up there.

While there's a lot more awareness of the AIDS epidemic today than there was even five years ago, due in large measure to the courageous actions of athletes such as Magic Johnson and Arthur Ashe, our administration and all citizens need to do much, much more. We respond quickly in sudden disasters such as earthquakes and hurricanes, which rip through communities and leave devastation behind, but we're so much slower in reacting to this epidemic, which will kill tens of millions before it's contained. We must put aside our personal feelings about drug abuse and homosexuality, and recognize that the effect of AIDS is the same as a hurricane. Our brothers and sisters are dying, and their dignity is being sacrificed as well.

I can only hope that the day is not far off when this horrible disease doesn't have to be a source of shame to those who suffer and die from it.

*   *   *

Our family struggled for quite a while after Paul's death to make sense of what had happened. I knew that all I could do was try to honor his life by carrying forward with the message he'd given me: just to be myself and go out and win.

While I hadn't won on the PGA Tour since 1984, I had been close on several occasions. I'd had something like seven runnerup finishes in the past five years. But I won the Isuzu Kapalua International in November of 1989, and then, in a victory that was extra-special, I won the Bob Hope Chrysler Classic two months later, playing the final round on the PGA West/Palmer Course. Coincidentally, the last round of golf I'd ever played with Paul was sixteen months before on that very course. My dad was also with us.

I struggled with that realization the entire last round. I was paired with Steve Elkington and Mike Reid, and had a two-shot lead, but I was also wrestling with vivid memories of playing the Palmer course with Paul and Dad. Every time my mind would wander and I would think about Paul, I'd hear him say, "Don't think about me. I'm fine. Just go out and win." That thought carried me all day.

When I birdied the last hole to win, David, who had come to Palm Springs for the week, gave me a big hug, and I said, "I sure wish Dad and Paul were here to see this."

And David said, "Paul saw every shot. I think he helped you keep that last three-iron on line."

Then all of a sudden I was surrounded by media, and presented the crystal by Bob and Dolores Hope, and flash bulbs were popping and a big check was being held up, and all the other hoopla was taking place that goes with a victory. But inside I still had all these sad, quiet thoughts that I couldn't talk about. I did mention Paul briefly in the press conference, but I shared only a small part of what was on my mind.

I waited until now to tell the rest.

Afterword

ALTHOUGH SOME PEOPLE may see the game of golf as repetitious—chasing a stupid ball with a stick—or intrusive, as in Mark Twain's definition, "Golf is a good walk spoiled," I find it endlessly fascinating. You never hit the same shot twice in your life. A four-foot putt from the identical spot may move differently in the afternoon than in the morning because of the shadows, or the traffic that's passed through in the interim.

Like life, golf is a constant struggle, but the mistakes we make are really just opportunities to learn and grow. Bruce Cudd, a former Walker Cup player and touring professional from Portland, told me when I joined the Tour, "Peter, remember never to look back when you've finished a tournament. Simply sign the card, cash your check, and move on. Rehashing missed opportunities will only eat you alive."

I've tried to follow Bruce's advice, and shake off adversity in pursuit of a better tomorrow. I've also remembered my father's last comment to me, that humor is the most important part of golf.

This book has provided an opportunity for me to reflect

on hundreds of memorable moments in my life, and made
me realize the large debt of gratitude I owe to so many
people.

Thanks first to all the professional golfers who came
before me, whose skill and charisma made the PGA Tour
the wonderful traveling show it is today. Thanks also to the
many people who've helped me pursue my dreams.

I'd like to thank Hughes Norton, my manager, for taking a gamble on an unknown kid from Oregon.

Also, a nod to all those knowledgeable golf professionals
who were instrumental in the development of my game:

Jack Doss, the former head pro at Waverley, was always
willing to work with me as a junior player, to help me
develop good swing habits and reinforce positive thinking.
Every time I had a competition, Jack was willing to watch
me hit balls beforehand, and keep my mind on track. He
had a courteous, classy style that demonstrated great pride
in his profession.

I learned a great deal from a professional named Marlow
Quick, the head pro at Astoria Country Club on the Oregon coast where we spent our summers. Marlow was the
consummate club pro: a good instructor, a really fine
player, a great storyteller, and even a trick-shot artist.
Mostly, I remember that Marlow always made golf fun,
something for which I'm greatly indebted to him today.

All kids have somebody they look up to and say, gee, I
wonder if I could ever be that good. For me, that was Pat
Fitzsimons, who as a young player from Salem, Oregon,
won everything in sight. I remember distinctly when I was
about fourteen, watching Fitz and Bob Duden walking
down an adjacent fairway with a loyal gallery braving the
rains. Duden had won the Oregon Open so many times
they'd lost count, and here was this seventeen-year-old kid
with red hair and glasses beating him in a head-to-head

showdown. I though that was just awesome, that a kid just a little older than myself could whip all the best players in the area and win the state open. I remember feeling a little ache in my stomach, which were the seeds of a desire to improve my own game and see if I could ever get that good.

It's great how things work out sometimes. Now Pat Fitzsimons is a good friend and the head pro of our new course, the Oregon Golf Club.

But I'll always look at him and see that seventeen-year-old kid who was able to whip the old pro.

And there were so many others: Buck McKendrick, Jon Peterson, Claude Harmon, Dick Harmon, Bob Ellsworth, Jerry Mowlds, Mike Davis, Tim Berg, Jimmy Ballard, John Rhodes, David Leadbetter, Joanne Beddow, Randy Henry, Ross Henry, Bob Torrance, Jim McLean, Dave Glenz, Jim Hardy, Carol Mann, Dave Pelz, and Pat Rielly.

My gratitude also to my original sponsors: Peter Murphy, Don McKellar, Norm Parsons, Gay Davis, Mark Johnson, Ed Stanley, Bill Swindells, Jr., Harry Kane, Maury Pruitt, Will Gonyea, J. H. Gonyea, Bob Wilhelm, John Tennant, Bob Benjamin, Bill Kilkenny, and Rich Guggenheim.

A big thank-you to Bob McCurry, Vice-Chairman of Toyota Motor Sales U.S.A., who was so kind to me during the latter stages of my father's illness. Thanks also to Phil Knight of Nike for his belief in golf. And to Ben Bidwell, my partner in the Chrysler Team Championship days and a charter member of team "No-Name." And to Dennis Rose and Thos Rohr at Waikoloa Resort, for a slice of heaven.

Thanks to my mother, Barbara, for her love and support of all my endeavors, no matter how offbeat. And to Annabelle and Esley Davis, the greatest in-laws a guy could have.

Most importantly, thanks to Jan, who is everything to me—my wife, my lover, my best friend, and the perfect mother to our children. Thanks for your love, respect, patience, and understanding. I couldn't have done any of it without you.

To Amy, Kristen and Mickey, thanks for understanding your old man's obsession with a silly game.

And finally, a special thanks to my friend Chuck Hogan, who has taken my most stubborn muscle—my brain—and gotten it in sync. I can still consistently hole invisible putts from ten feet.

Gunga-la-Gunga.